HOW TO PLAN AND BUILD

FENCES & GATES

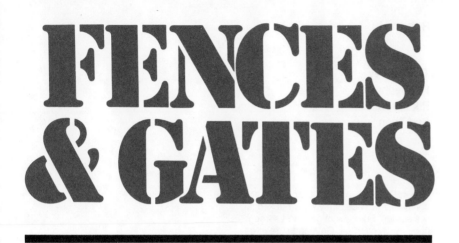

BY THE EDITORS OF SUNSET BOOKS
AND SUNSET MAGAZINE

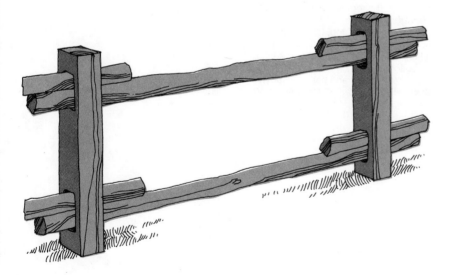

LANE PUBLISHING CO.

MENLO PARK, CALIFORNIA

Foreword

Fences, gates, and garden screens are such a familiar part of most landscapes that we rarely focus on them—until we decide to build one. To the prospective builder, the diversity of these structures then becomes readily apparent.

But which one will best suit *your* needs? This book will answer that question and many more: it is a complete guide to planning and building fences, gates, and garden screens to suit a wide range of circumstances and needs. You'll also find information on fence and gate repair, as well as ideas for fence decoration and plantings.

We'd like to say thanks . . .

. . . to the many homeowners who let us photograph their fences, screens, and gates, and to the landscape architects, designers, and fence contractors who showed us their work.

We also appreciate the contributions of the following individuals who shared their technical expertise: Ken Slusser, Pacific Fence Co.; Jack Belick; William Louis Kapranos; Gene Kunit; Richard Murray; and John Sullivan. Finally, special thanks go to the California Redwood Association and the Jordan International Company for their valuable assistance.

Editor, Sunset Books: David E. Clark

Second printing September 1982

Staff Editors:
James Barrett
Don Rutherford

Design:
Robert Hu

Illustrations:
Tom Hickey
Bill Oetinger
Rik Olson
Bud Thon

Cover: Diagonal siding of Dutch gate complements lines of plywood-backed lattice screen. Full view of gate and screen appears on page 44. Gate and screen design: Richard Murray. Photograph: Ells Marugg. Cover design: Zan Fox.

Photographers

James Barrett: 21 top. **René Klein:** 18. **Jack McDowell:** 19 center and bottom, 20 top, 21 center, 23 top, 24, 25 bottom, 26, 28 bottom, 31, 32 bottom left, 34 bottom, 35 bottom, 39 bottom, 43 center and bottom, 44 top, 47 top. **Steve W. Marley:** 19 top, 22 bottom, 27 bottom, 28 top, 36 37 top, 38 bottom, 39 top and center, 41 bottom, 42 bottom, 44 bottom, 45. **Ells Marugg:** 20 bottom, 21 bottom, 22 top, 23 bottom, 25 top, 27 top, 28 bottom, 29, 30 bottom, 32 top and bottom right, 33, 34 top left and right, 35 top and center, 37 bottom, 40 bottom, 41 top, 42 top, 43 top, 46, 47 center and bottom. **Robyn Shotwell:** 27 center, 30 top, 38 top, 40 top.

CONTENTS

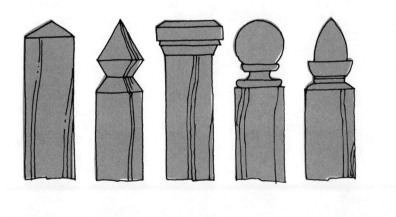

PLANNING FENCES & SCREENS

- **Fences and outdoor screens: what they can do for you**
- **Regulations that govern fence building**
- **Choosing fence materials**
- **Lumber used in fencing**

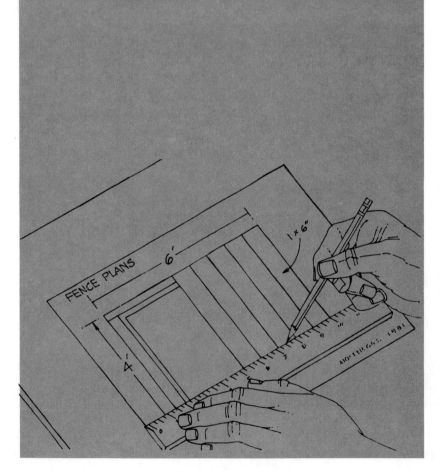

There are always two sides to every fence: the inside and the out-side, your side and your neighbor's side, a functional side and an esthetic side. No matter what type of fence you choose to build, care-ful planning will make the grass look greener on both sides.

Whether you're confronting a nude yard, with a blushingly clear view of neighboring houses, or planning to dress up a mature ex-isting landscape, certain fence planning considerations remain the same. In all cases, you'll be faced with the following questions:

• What purposes do you expect the fence to serve? (Among the possibilities: define a boundary, offer protection and privacy, con-trol sun and wind.)

• Which type of fence best fits the surrounding landscape and architecture?

• Where will the fence go?

• What materials will be used to build the fence?

• Will the chosen fence design and location meet local codes and ordinances?

• Who will design and build the fence?

• How much will it cost?

This chapter will help you an-swer these and other planning questions and will guide you through the steps necessary in planning a successful project.

Outdoor screens. You'll notice that fences and outdoor screens are discussed synonymously throughout much of this chapter—that's because both require many of the same planning considera-tions.

Outdoor screens are simply high, lightweight sections of fence, either freestanding or acting as partial walls around patios, decks, and other outdoor spaces. They serve many of the same functions as a tall fence—when made of lath, plastic or glass panels, or other lightweight screening material, out-door screens can provide privacy, block unwanted views, or alleviate wind and sun problems. An out-

POPULAR FENCE STYLES

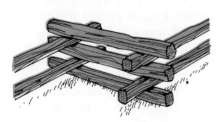

Split rail (zigzag)

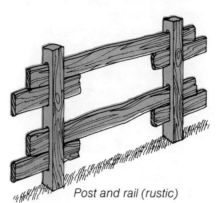

Post and rail (rustic)

4 × 4

Post and rail (formal)

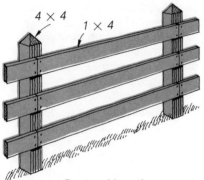

4 × 4 1 × 4

Post and board

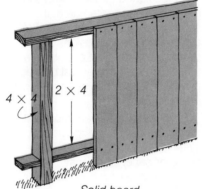

4 × 4 2 × 4

Solid board

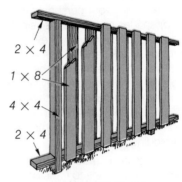

2 × 4
1 × 8
4 × 4
2 × 4

Alternate board

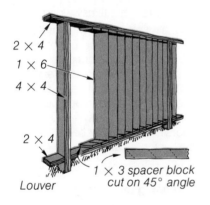

2 × 4
1 × 6
4 × 4
2 × 4
1 × 3 spacer block
cut on 45° angle

Louver

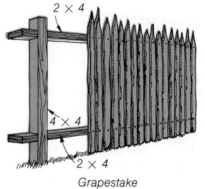

2 × 4
4 × 4
2 × 4

Grapestake

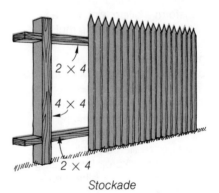

2 × 4
4 × 4
2 × 4

Stockade

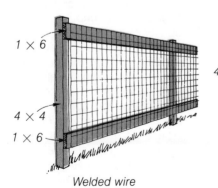

1 × 6
4 × 4
1 × 6

Welded wire

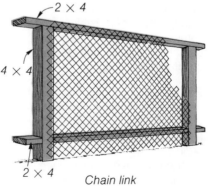

2 × 4
4 × 4
2 × 4

Chain link

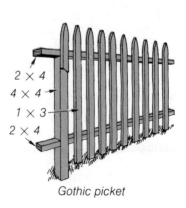

2 × 4
4 × 4
1 × 3
2 × 4

Gothic picket

door screen becomes a fence only when it encloses a large section of property, such as a back yard.

Examples of outdoor screens appear on pages 38 through 43 in the color section of this book. Detailed building techniques appear on pages 48–60 and 68–79.

FENCES AND OUTDOOR SCREENS: WHAT THEY CAN DO FOR YOU

In the cheek- by-jowl closeness of modern living, our personal outdoor spaces become increasingly valuable for the privacy they can provide. Back yards become havens where family members find solace, pursue leisure activities, and entertain guests; front yards become reflections of their owners—from congenially inviting to outright forbidding.

Fences and outdoor screens provide the means to transform a naked yard into a secure, attractive retreat from the outside world. Well designed, they filter the sun's glare, transform a biting wind into a pleasant zephyr, or help mute the cacophony of street traffic, noisy neighbors, and barking dogs. As partitions, they divide the yard into separate areas for recreation, relaxation, gardening, and storage.

Many fences and screens are designed to provide support for vines or espaliered plants, or to serve as a backdrop for planting beds, trelliswork, or other garden structures.

Labeled drawings of popular fence styles appear on page 5. They'll help you understand some of the terms used throughout this book.

Fencing for protection

Since earliest times, the primary role of fencing has been to protect life and property from human and animal invaders. That early use of fences to protect crops and livestock can be translated into the modern context of protecting gardens and pets.

Our ancestors also relied on fences for security or for discouraging trespassers—a use that has gained renewed importance in recent years. The stockade fence used by pioneers to enclose forts and settlements is an early example of security fencing. A smaller version of this time-tested design is popular for residential security today.

In the broadest sense of the term, security fencing includes any fence designed to keep people in or out of a designated area; it should be tall, sturdy, and hard to climb. Many fence designs fit this description; the most popular are those using 1-inch vertical boards, plywood panels, heavy-gauge wire mesh, or chain link.

Psychology plays an important part in the design of a good security fence. For example, a solid board or panel fence may be a more effective psychological deterrent than a chain link fence, simply because the would-be intruder can't see what's on the other side.

Protecting children. Security fencing can contain children within an area such as a play yard. The type of fence you choose for this purpose will depend on your child's age and fence-climbing ability. A basketweave fence, for instance, makes a perfect stepladder, and a 2 by 4-inch wire mesh fence is easily scaled by small hands and feet.

So, like other kinds of security fencing, a child- proof fence should be high and sturdy and should provide no toeholds. Smaller wire mesh (2 by 2-inch) is ideal for play yards—its open design allows parents to keep an eye on their children's activities.

Pool fencing. Many communities require fences around swimming pools to protect children and non-swimmers. Even if there's no such ordinance in your area, your insurance company may require you to fence your pool in order to qualify for a homeowner's policy. In most cases, the fence must be at least 6 feet tall and must meet local code requirements for design and materials. For examples of pool fencing, see pages 20 and 31.

Containing animals. In rural areas, fences are required to keep livestock from straying and ruining neighbors' crops. Ranchers and farmers are familiar with these types of fences and know how to build them.

As more suburbanites move to the country and find that they can keep a few horses, chickens, or other livestock on their property, they need to know about these fence types. Though most weekend farmers don't have to worry about enclosing miles of land, the requirements for containing animals still apply.

Pet owners, too, are responsible for the actions of their animals. If you're keeping a dog on your property, you'll want to give special consideration to the fence design. Though few dogs can climb or jump a 6-foot fence, most can dig under one, and large dogs can break through a flimsy wood fence.

Chain link, heavy wire, or solid panels set in a ribbon of concrete will prevent dogs from gnawing through or digging underneath. Metal fencing is preferable to wood, because it is not damaged by scratching and gnawing. Of course, there hasn't been a fence built yet that can contain a cat!

Screening for privacy

The most effective privacy fences and screens are those you can't see over, under, around, or through. But you'll want to give some forethought to the design and location, to avoid the feeling of a boxed-in space. You can always break the monotony of a solid barrier by changing the face treatment of alternating sections (for example, the size or direction of boards and the color of panels).

A series of high-low or open-and-closed sections can block unwanted views (and peering neighbors) while preserving desirable sights beyond the yard. For instance, you can use solid sections where you want to block the line of sight, and open sections of transparent glass or plastic, wire, or spaced boards or pickets where you want a view.

Translucent glass or plastic panels can be used to allow light into the yard, yet obscure vision.

A louver fence can be very effective in blocking a view while allowing air circulation within the yard. Placed horizontally, louvers will shut out a view completely; placed vertically, they allow only a small section of the yard to be seen by anyone walking along the fence line.

Examples of privacy fences and screens appear on pages 20–21, 24–28, 34–35, 37, and 39–43.

Defining outdoor spaces

As outdoor living space becomes scarcer, many homeowners are seeking ways to make full use of yard areas. Used within the yard, fences and screens can delineate areas for work, recreation, relaxation, storage, and garden.

Low or open fences can physically separate areas while visually preserving the overall size of the yard. You can use taller screens to hide unattractive sights, such as trash or service areas, garden work centers, or swimming pool equipment. Where added security is required, choose chain link fencing with lath or metal inserts woven into the chain link (see drawing on page 14).

Tempering wind, sun, and noise

A fence or screen can effectively control the elements of wind and sun to create a pleasant environment in your yard. To achieve this, you'll first need to study how the sun and wind affect your property at various times of the year; then plan fence design and location accordingly.

Outside noise, too, can be controlled to some extent by solid fences and screens.

Wind control. As a rule, a solid barrier provides little wind protection across large expanses of yard—the wind simply vaults over it and continues at the same velocity a few feet downwind of the barrier. Tests have shown, though, that a wind screen or fence with an open design (spaced boards or slats, louvers, or woven lath) breaks up a steady wind into a series of eddies or small breezes. Compared with the effect of a solid fence, this action protects a larger area behind the fence or wind screen from the main force of the wind. The drawings to the right show the effects that several fence designs have on breaking up wind.

Sun control. Fences and screens can be designed to admit full sunlight, provide partial shade, or admit no sun at all on their shady sides. Transparent glass or plastic screens admit the maximum amount of light and a clear view while offering wind protection around patios and decks. To protect larger areas from wind, you'll need an open fence or screen design, as discussed above. You can reduce heat and glare from the sun by using tinted or glare-reducing glass or plastic, which cuts the intensity of the sun's rays, yet allows a view beyond.

Translucent glass or plastic panels of varying densities admit light while obscuring vision. Available in a variety of colors, patterns, and textures, these panels can make an attractive addition to the yard. Latticework or other open designs provide partial or filtered shade, necessary for the growth of many types of plants.

Noise control. When it comes to muting noise, one rule always applies—the thicker or higher the barrier, the more effective it will be. It should also have a solid, unbroken surface; joints between boards or panels must be tight fitting or covered with lath strips.

Of course, there are practical

SCREENING AGAINST THE WIND

(Degrees, showing rise in comfort temperature, are expressed in Fahrenheit)

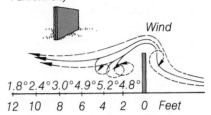

1.8° 2.4° 3.0° 4.9° 5.2° 4.8°
12 10 8 6 4 2 0 Feet

Wind washes over a solid fence as a stream of water washes over a solid barrier. Protection diminishes considerably at a distance about equal to the height of the fence.

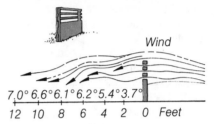

7.0° 6.6° 6.1° 6.2° 5.4° 3.7°
12 10 8 6 4 2 0 Feet

Spaced slats, either horizontal or vertical, break up wind flow. Up close, the fence offers less protection; temperatures are warmest 6' to 12' away.

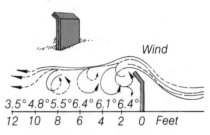

3.5° 4.8° 5.5° 6.4° 6.1° 6.4°
12 10 8 6 4 2 0 Feet

A 45° baffle at top of fence diverts downward crash of wind. You feel warmest in the pocket directly below the baffle and up to 8' away from the 6'-high fence.

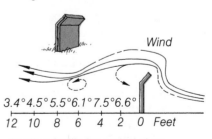

3.4° 4.5° 5.5° 6.1° 7.5° 6.6°
12 10 8 6 4 2 0 Feet

Angling baffle into wind gives greatest protection close to the fence, but effective protection extends to a distance equal to about twice the fence height.

limits to the height and thickness of a fence or outdoor screen (a solid masonry wall actually works best of all in cutting off noise). But there is a psychological advantage in *visually* cutting off the source of the noise: though the actual noise level may be reduced only slightly by a fence or screen, it will seem quieter if the receiver doesn't see the source of the noise.

Fences as landscaping tools

Fences and plants go together naturally. Fences and outdoor screens can be designed to support vines and espaliers (shrubs or trees trained to grow against the fence) or to act as a backdrop for planting beds. In turn, plants you've selected carefully can soften the stark expanse of a bare fence and add depth to its two-dimensional character.

Fences and screens can also be used as climate modifiers in your garden—to break a prevailing wind or to cast shade in areas where you want shade-loving plants to grow.

Plan the type and location of your plantings at the same time you're designing a new fence or screen. Keep the fence in scale with existing landscaping, and choose new plantings that will be in scale with the fence when they grow to mature size and shape.

The color and texture of a fence can also complement the color and texture of the plantings against it, when you plan a harmonious relationship: for instance, dark fences contrast pleasingly with light foliage and blooms. With light-colored fences, the reverse is true—an example is the traditional, striking combination of red roses backed by a white picket fence.

Fences and screens can also serve as a support or backdrop for other planting structures, such as trellises, raised planter boxes, hanging planters, or potting sheds.

For more detailed information on planting around fences and outdoor screens, see pages 84–87.

REGULATIONS GOVERNING FENCING

Before you make any specific plans for the size, design, and location of your fence or outdoor screen, look into the local codes and ordinances that may influence these decisions. Requirements and restrictions will vary considerably from state to state, city to city, and even neighborhood to neighborhood.

There are regulations covering many different fencing situations. Restrictions on barbed wire, electric fencing, glass, and other materials of a hazardous nature are almost universal. And there are various ordinances limiting the height of front and back-yard boundary fences and fences situated near traffic intersections. In addition to height restrictions, there are likely to be code-imposed setback distances from buildings, property lines, or the street to affect the intended location of your fence or screen.

Fence height

Most communities have height restrictions on boundary or division fencing. These restrictions may vary somewhat from one community to the next. Generally, though, front-yard fencing is limited to 4 feet in height, back-yard fencing to 6 to 8 feet. Some communities allow the standard fence height to be exceeded, if the extended portion is composed of wire mesh, lattice, or other open work.

Fences that border intersections or sharp bends in the street must meet certain height restrictions and setback distances from the street. The reason for these restrictions is to allow motorists an unobstructed view of oncoming traffic.

In all such matters, though, never assume—always check with local authorities about fence height and setback distances. In the event that your plans do conflict with local regulations, you may be able to obtain a variance.

Use of hazardous materials

Though security has become a major consideration in many urban and suburban areas, using any fence material intended to cut, impale, or otherwise injure can result in serious lawsuits and is therefore restricted in most residential communities. Most local codes are fairly specific on hazardous materials and their uses. Materials such as barbed wire and electrified fencing are usually restricted to farm, commercial, and industrial uses. Glass used in fencing must be tempered safety glass rather than ordinary window glass.

Boundary and division fences

From the time the first fence was built to define a property line, such barriers have provoked many a dispute, both in and out of court. Even if the fence is built to resolve land ownership disagreement, problems can arise concerning fence ownership and maintenance. To help minimize these and other potential conflicts, it's wise to make a written agreement with your present neighbors concerning fence design and location; if possible, try to enlist their active cooperation in building the fence. Even if you can't get your neighbors' help, you should be aware of the following:

Who owns it? Fences are generally considered to belong to the land on which they're built—but a boundary or division fence belongs to adjoining property owners as tenants in common. To avoid ownership disputes, you'll need an accurate survey of the boundary to be sure the fence is correctly placed.

Who's responsible? If you're building a fence directly on the property line, make a *written* agreement with the adjoining landowner(s) in advance, specifying location and type of fence, and dividing the responsibility for building and maintaining it. If possible, have the agreement recorded at the city or county clerk's office to avoid future ownership disputes, should either of the properties change hands.

Of course, it's not always possible to get your neighbors' cooperation, especially in the case of a ''spite fence.'' If built on the property line, the fence belongs both to you and to the adjoining landowners, though they are under no obligation to help build it, pay for it, or even maintain it, unless that written agreement has been made.

The neighbors' only obligation is to refrain from defacing or destroying the fence intentionally—and this, of course, doesn't take into account poor taste in colors, should the neighbors decide to paint their side.

One solution to this problem is to build the fence at least 6 inches in from your side of the property line—then you need not consult the neighbors on its construction or maintenance. But this method offers no assurance that your neighbors won't resent the fence, or you for building it.

Another way to avoid ill feelings is to build a fence that looks as good on the neighbors' side as on yours. Still, the best solution is to seek a reasonable amount of cooperation.

Required fencing

Fence laws and codes not only restrict and regulate the type of fence you build, but also may *require* you to erect a fence in certain instances. For example, many communities require protective fences to enclose swimming pools or to contain livestock or pets. Open wells, excavations, and other potentially dangerous situations on your property may also require fencing.

Sources of information

The most obvious source of information on fence codes and restrictions is your local building department or community planning office. Fence contractors are also familiar with local codes and building practices and apply them in their work.

It's important not to make assumptions or to rely on information given by neighbors. For example, it's not safe to assume that a new fence is a proper one just because it is similar to existing fences in the neighborhood—new zoning ordinances may have been passed since the older fences were built. Always seek advice from local authorities before erecting any fence or outdoor screen.

DESIGNING YOUR FENCE

Once you've chosen a basic type of fence to suit your needs and have roughly determined its location on the property, it's time to plan the details.

The overall appearance of your fence will depend not only on the basic style you've chosen but also on its actual dimensions (height, post spacing, lumber dimensions), the materials used in its construction, and the characteristics of the property on which it sits. All of these design elements must harmonize to form a functional and attractive structure.

With careful planning, you can also save on materials, without sacrificing quality. Some designs that use fewer materials than others may be perfectly adequate for your needs. You may also be able to use a less expensive type of siding with good results. Designing your fence to make the best use of standard lumber lengths also saves time and money (see ''Drawing up your plans,'' at right). Depending on the complexity of your project, you might save money in the long run by hiring a professional to design the fence.

Studying your property

Your first design consideration will be the actual site on which the fence is to be built. Take into account lot size, shape, and grade, sun orientation, wind direction, and the characteristics of surrounding structures and plantings.

The best way to learn more about your property is to obtain a plot or site plan, if you don't already have one. Architects' drawings often include an overall site plan along with the house plans; here you'll find the lot size, shape, grade, and orientation to north along with the house size and location. If yours is an architect-designed house, you can get these plans from the architect; if not, try the developer or the contractor who built the house, or possibly a previous owner.

If the property was professionally landscaped, the landscape architect who did the work should be able to supply you with a detailed site plan showing planting locations relative to the lot.

Deed maps show the actual dimensions and orientations of the site. They're available through your city hall or county courthouse, from the title company, or from the bank putting out the loan on the house.

Drawing up your plans

Fence projects, large and small, should be planned on paper. This will allow you to think out the entire project in advance and experiment with various ideas, costing you no more than the price of a pencil and a few sheets of paper. In addition to helping you estimate materials, the drawings will enable you to visualize the effect the fence will have on the overall landscaping scheme.

You can save money and avoid wasting material if you design your fence to make the best use of standard lumber lengths (lengths are in multiples of 2 feet). For instance, posts spaced 4, 6, or 8 feet from center of one post to the center of the next make the best use of lumber for rails and kick boards. To avoid waste and unnecessary cutting of siding materials, round off fence height to the nearest foot.

The scale drawing. The first step in drawing up your plans is to make an accurate scale drawing of the property, or of the portion of the property where the fence or screen will go.

Use the site plan as a guide, and make your scale drawing on a large sheet of ¼-inch graph paper (*scale ¼ inch = 1 foot*). Include the following features:

1. Overall dimensions of the lot

2. Location of the house and other existing structures

3. Direction of north

4. Path of the sun

5. Direction of prevailing wind

6. Setback distances and easements from buildings, property lines, and the street (available from your local building department)

7. Existing plantings

8. Any problems beyond the lot that may affect sun, view, or privacy.

A sample scale drawing is shown below.

Once your lot drawing is complete, lay a sheet of tracing paper over it and sketch various fence ideas. If the fence comes as part of an overall landscaping project, include the sizes and locations to proposed plantings and structures. When you've come up with an overall landscape plan, you're ready to make a detailed drawing of the fence layout by itself on a tracing paper overlay.

Next, make an accurate elevation drawing of one or two sections of fence to help you visualize your design and to help you estimate quantities of materials later. Your drawing should be dimensioned to show post spacing, sizes of lumber or other fence material, and overall dimensions of posts, rails, and siding. The drawing below is an example of such an elevation drawing (for a solid board fence). See page 5 for other fence designs.

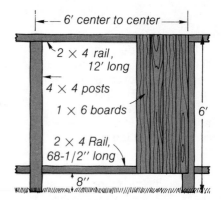

Elevation drawing *helps you visualize design and estimate fence materials.*

SCALE DRAWING

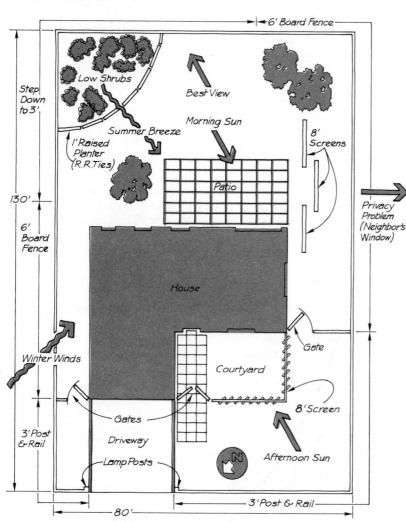

Solving layout problems

If every lot were free of obstruction, smooth as a baseball diamond, and measured in even increments of 6 or 8 feet, laying out a fence over its surface would be very simple. But often the fence planner must figure out how to get the fence around a tree, up a slope, or across a ditch or depression. Or your fence or screen may require one or more curved sections. Problems like these may call for a professional hand, but here are some suggestions that may help you.

Hillside fencing. If your fence line runs uphill, there are two basic ways you can lay out the fence: one is to follow the natural contours of the land, and the other is to lay the fence out in steps. The method you use will depend on both the basic design and the materials that you'll choose for your fence.

Some designs that adapt especially well to contour fencing are post-and-rail fences, or solid fences using pickets, palings, or grapestakes (see drawing below).

Stepped fences, more geometric in form, are more difficult to design and build, but they are preferred in populous areas, where the strong horizontal and vertical lines of the fence complement the geometric lines of surrounding houses. Solid board, louver, basketweave, and panel fences are at their best when laid out in stepped sections.

In either stepped or contoured fencing, the bottoms of boards 6 inches or wider should be cut to follow the contour of the hillside; otherwise, triangular gaps will result where the fence siding meets the ground, giving animals easier access and providing an unfinished appearance. Examples of stepped and contour fencing are shown below.

Contour fencing

This　*Not this*

Stepped fencing

For tips on plotting hillside fences, see page 52.

Dealing with trees.　Sometimes fence layout can be complicated by one or more trees growing in the path of the fence line. You have three alternatives: you can remove the tree, relocate the fence, or make the tree part of the fence.

To do the latter, install posts several feet from either side of the trunk (so that no damage is done to the tree's root system) and extend the fence to within a few inches of the trunk, as shown in the drawing below. The fence edge should be far enough away to allow the contour of the tree trunk to change over the years.

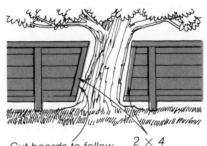

Cut boards to follow trunk angle　*2 × 4*

Don't attach the fence to the tree in any way—nails or screws driven into the trunk allow bacteria and disease to enter. Similarly, wire or other materials wrapped around the trunk would eventually restrict the flow of sap, injuring or killing the tree.

Curved fencing.　There are two ways to design a curved fence—along a true arc or in short, straight sections angled to form an arc. To secure a true arc, you can use a railless (or "palisade") fence. Or you can curve the top and bottom rails by laminating pieces of benderboard or, for a shallow arc, 1 by 4 pieces of decay-resistant lumber (see drawing above right).

The other choice, bringing the fence around in a series of short chords or sections (drawing above right), works best for designs using

CURVED FENCING

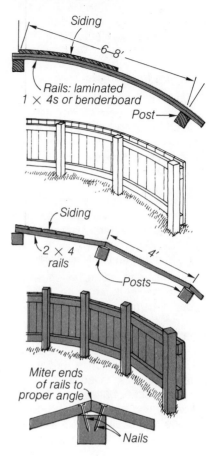

Siding　*6–8'*

Rails: laminated 1 × 4s or benderboard　*Post*

Siding

2 × 4 rails　*4'*

Posts

Miter ends of rails to proper angle　*Nails*

panels or rails. This last method must be used for wire fences, as wire cannot be pulled under tension around a curve.

Instructions for plotting a curved fence are on pages 51–52.

Skirting a bank.　When the fence has to be built along the edge of a bank, bluff, or cliff, it's a good idea to enlist the aid of a landscape architect or an engineer. Either should be able to tell you just how close to the edge the fence can be without eventually being lost to erosion. Posts must generally be sunk deeper than usual to accommodate shifting of soil.

Often plantings along the bank will check soil erosion, but in some cases a retaining wall must be used. For more on the subject of retaining walls, see the *Sunset* books *Walks, Walls & Patio Floors* and *Basic Masonry Illustrated.*

Fences built atop retaining walls have posts fastened to the masonry with post anchors or angle brackets.

Planning for the gate

If your fence plan includes a gate, you'll have two decisions to make: where the gate will go, and how it will be designed. Choosing the location should be fairly simple—gates are located for convenience. Study your present garden scheme, giving consideration to proposed additions or changes that may affect traffic through the yard. Then decide where the gate or gates best fit into the fence line.

The gate can match the fence in appearance, or it can be an attention-getter in a contrasting size, design, or material, or a combination of these elements. You can either buy a ready-built gate or build one yourself. Once you've determined the location and basic design, decide what size the gate will be so you can determine post spacing and location (posts for gates must often be more substantial than fence-line posts). For complete planning and building details for gates, see pages 88–95.

Where to get design help

If you need assistance in designing your fence, there are several ways to go about it. The most complete and unified design is likely to come from a landscape architect or landscape designer, who will plan the whole garden scheme with the fence integral to it. This, of course, is also the most expensive way to go and is usually necessary only if you are engaging in a major landscaping project.

If you merely need advice on specific designing problems, you can work with a landscape architect or designer on a per-hour consultation basis. In some cases, you may want one to have a set of plans drawn up, for a specified fee.

Landscape architects are state-licensed professionals with a degree in landscape architecture. They're trained in both the esthetics and the structural details of landscape design. If hired to do the entire project, the architect will provide a complete set of plans, negotiate bids from contractors, and supervise construction.

Landscape designers have varied experience and training in landscape design; they are not required to have the state license of a landscape architect. Most do have a landscape contractor's license and provide both design and installation services.

Fence contractors are also capable of helping you with design problems, but their experience tends to be more with structure than with esthetics. Some may be reluctant to offer too much free advice unless assured of the job of building your fence.

Whether you choose a landscape architect, a landscape designer, or a fence contractor to help with design or to do the actual design and building, first examine the professional's previous work, concerning yourself with quality and whether or not the person's tastes parallel your own.

Don't overlook the wide variety of prefabricated fence design in wood, metals, and other materials. Most manufacturers of prefab fencing provide brochures and other information on the various applications of their fencing, along with installation instructions. Prefab fencing can be obtained from fence dealers, lumber suppliers, and home improvement centers, or directly from the manufacturer. Look in the Yellow Pages under "Fence Materials."

Working with a contractor

If you decide to have a fence or landscape contractor build your fence, you'll naturally want one who does quality work and then stands behind it. Your choice should be based on the individual's reputation as a fence builder rather than the lowest bid, though low bids and inferior work don't always go hand in hand.

Select a contractor who's cooperative, competent, financially secure (check bank and credit references), and well established in the community. Reputable licensed contractors are also insured for property damage, public liability, and workers' compensation, for their own legal protection and yours.

Unless you've had prior experience with a good contractor or have been referred to one by a reliable source, you'll have to do some careful research to find one. The best place to start is the phone book under the heading "Fence Contractors." Your best bet is to stick with the smaller contractors specializing in custom residential fencing, since larger contractors rarely take on small jobs and often have work scheduled months in advance.

Always get at least three competitive bids for the job, and ask to see examples of the contractor's work before making your choice.

The contractor's estimates should include a complete list of materials and price breakdowns. Because prices of materials and labor are continually rising, the contractor often reserves the right to withdraw the estimate, after an agreed-upon period, if the bid is not accepted.

The contract. Once you've chosen a contractor, the next step is to draw up a solid contract that includes detailed drawings and descriptions of all work to be done, a description of materials to be used (lumber species and grades, hardware and fasteners, finishes, and so forth), a time schedule, a firm price, and terms of payment.

Building it yourself

Fence building is not technically difficult, though the work is often physically demanding. For this reason it's wise to have someone work with you on the actual construction, especially when you're setting and aligning fence posts. Ask a friend or neighbor to help, or hire a laborer when needed.

The first step will be to apply for a building permit, if one is required. Then make your materials list and begin shopping for materials; the following section will help you select them. Actual building techniques for fences start on page 48 and for gates on page 88. You'll also find construction details for a number of specific fence and outdoor screen designs, starting on page 61.

CHOOSING FENCE MATERIALS

In most cases when people say "fence," they're thinking "wood." Most of us are also familiar with fences made of wrought iron, wire, and chain link. But a number of other materials—such as glass, plastics, fiberglass, aluminum, and masonry materials—are also suitable for fence and outdoor screen construction.

Common fence materials and their applications are discussed here. Specific fence and screen designs employing these materials are featured in the chapter "Projects," starting on page 61. Other suitable fence materials are limited only by the imagination of the user, provided they are structurally stable and weather resistant.

No matter which building materials you choose for posts, rails, and facing, you'll need fasteners—nails, screws, bolts, and brackets—to put them all together. Concrete mix, too, will be on your shopping list, as the posts of most fences should be set in concrete. See page 49 for details about hardware and concrete.

If you intend to apply a finish, order finishing materials—paint, stain, or clear finish (see page 59).

Wood

Most fences have wood in their construction, either totally or in concert with other materials. The versatility of wood as a fencing material is reflected in the seemingly limitless variety of its forms—split rails and grapestakes, dimension lumber, poles, and wood products like plywood and tempered hardboard.

Dimension lumber includes all wood cut to a specific thickness and width. The choice in lumber alone is so extensive that it is discussed separately on pages 15–17.

Split wood—rough split rails and grapestakes—is used for rustic-looking fences. *Poles* come in various sizes, from 3 to 12 inches or larger in diameter. You can buy poles either smooth-turned on a lathe to specific diameters, or in the rough, cut from saplings with bark and branches removed. Six-inch-diameter poles are most commonly used as fence posts; they're available pressure-treated with a preservative for that purpose. Smaller diameter poles, sometimes called palings, are used for stockade-type fencing.

Plywood and hardboard, used for panel fencing, are discussed below.

Plywood. An old standby for solid panel fences and screens, exterior-grade plywood comes in standard 4-foot-wide sheets, with 8, 10, and 12-foot lengths. Thicknesses range from $\frac{3}{8}$ inch to over 1 inch; the most common sizes used for fencing are $\frac{3}{8}$ inch, $\frac{1}{2}$ inch, $\frac{5}{8}$ inch, and $\frac{3}{4}$ inch. Surface texture can be smooth, rough-sawn, or grooved, or can simulate siding.

You can buy plywood unfinished, primed for painting, prestained in a variety of colors, or with a stucco or aggregate finish. Plywood is also used as a backing for wood and masonry facing materials.

Plywood panels under $\frac{3}{4}$ inch thick require bracing (the fence is framed like a wall in your house). Brace panels $\frac{3}{8}$ inch thick or less with 2 by 4 vertical studs, attached to top and bottom rails and spaced 16 inches on centers.

For panels $\frac{1}{2}$ to $\frac{5}{8}$ inch thick, space 2 by 4s 24 inches on centers. Panels $\frac{3}{4}$ inch or thicker require no bracing, but their weight makes it necessary to use sturdier posts and rails in the fence design.

Remember to select only exterior-grade plywood. The glue bonding the plies on interior-grade plywood won't hold up to the weather, and the plies will separate after a few seasons.

Hardboard. Several kinds of hardboard are on the market, but only tempered hardboard (smooth on both sides) is suitable for fencing. Made of wood fiber that is bonded under heat and pressure, tempered hardboard is quite heavy and quite strong—relatively thin panels can be used for fencing.

Tempered hardboard can be painted easily, but its medium to dark brown surface won't take a stain. It is available in standard 4-foot widths in lengths of 8 to 12 feet. It offers good resistance to weather and won't crack or split under normal conditions. Like most paneling materials, hardboard needs studs (vertical supports) between top and bottom rails to prevent bowing.

Wire

Next to wood, wire is perhaps the most versatile fencing material. It comes in welded or woven mesh, single strands (barbed wire or hog wire), poultry netting, and chain link (see drawing on next page). Wire for exterior use is made of galvanized steel, aluminum, or vinyl-coated metal; it's available in a number of gauges, mesh sizes, and roll lengths and widths.

Wire—one of the more economical forms of fencing—is useful for providing security, supporting plants and vines, enclosing play yards and animal pens, and protecting garden areas from small animals. Welded or woven mesh and chain link can be attached to a wood framework to form a light, sturdy, and attractive fence (for examples, see pages 42 and 76), or they can be installed as part of an all-metal fence.

WIRE FENCING TYPES

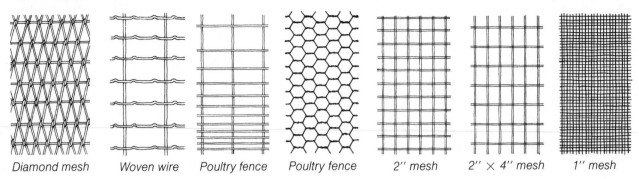

Diamond mesh   Woven wire   Poultry fence   Poultry fence   2" mesh   2" × 4" mesh   1" mesh

Chain link. Once considered a commercial and industrial fence material, chain link has become a feature in many residential landscapes. To relieve the stark, metallic look, vinyl-coated chain link fencing is available in several colors, most typically black, green, and white.

Also, wood lath or metal insert strips can be woven into the chain link to provide privacy and add interest to the fence. Metal inserts come in a variety of colors, which can be used artistically to create interesting pattern effects. The drawing below shows how strips are inserted in the chain link fencing.

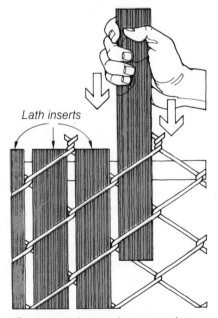

Lath inserts

Starting at the top, *insert wood or metal strips into the chain link fabric.*

Ornamental metal fencing

Not too many years ago, ornamental metal fencing meant ornamental iron—those elegant wrought iron masterpieces that graced the mansions of the Victorian era. Today, the term encompasses not only traditional wrought iron, but ornamental steel and aluminum as well. Designs in all three metals range from ornate hand-crafted works of art to sleek modern grillwork available in prefabricated sections.

Many ornamental iron fences from the past have been salvaged and restored to make attractive additions to today's gardens. But these antiques take some serious hunting and many painstaking hours to restore, making it more practical to have the fence fabricated by an iron worker or to buy a prefabricated design from an ornamental fencing manufacturer.

There are contractors who specialize in the installation of ornamental metal fences, because the job is somewhat complex. You can choose to hire such a contractor, or you can install prefabricated metal fence sections yourself by attaching them to wood posts (see page 31). This procedure requires precision work because each section must fit snugly between posts.

For custom-designed ornamental fences, look in the Yellow Pages under the heading "Iron Ornamental Work"; for prefabricated designs, look under the heading "Fence Materials."

Aluminum Fencing

Strength, durability, and ease of maintenance are positive features of prefabricated aluminum fencing. It is sold in sections that can be installed with either aluminum or wood posts. You assemble the fence with screwdrivers or wrenches rather than with hammer and nails—manufacturers provide assembly instructions as part of the package.

Designs include decorative panels, simulated wrought iron, and a variety of simulated wood styles, including picket, basketweave, and board.

Aluminum fencing comes in a number of baked enamel colors, so it need not be repainted as frequently as fences of other materials. Depending on the style, aluminum fencing is available in heights from 3 to 6 feet. (Several manufacturers offer similar fencing systems in galvanized steel.)

Plastic panels

Numerous kinds of plastic panels are available for use in fences and outdoor screens, but they boil down to two basic types: clear, glasslike acrylic panels, and translucent panels (known in the trade as "obscure" panels) in a number of colors, patterns, and surface textures, with varying degrees of light transmission.

Flat or corrugated "fiberglass" panels (actually made of fiberglass-reinforced polyester) can be used for translucent outdoor screens and patio overheads. These panels are somewhat artificial-looking and require careful screen design and selection of surrounding plantings.

Plastic panels are lightweight and difficult to break, but they are susceptible to abrasion and weather erosion; colored panels will fade in time if exposed to the sun. You'll find sources for plastic panels in the Yellow Pages under "Plastics—Rods, Tubes, Sheets, Etc., Supply Centers." The dealer can cut plastic panels to the size you need.

Masonry materials

Though we usually associate masonry materials—brick, stone, concrete, and so forth—with walls rather than fences, some of these materials do have applications in fencing.

One example is the stucco fence. It resembles a wall, but you can build it in the same manner as an ordinary fence: set wood posts, and attach wood rails and exterior plywood siding. Stucco is then applied to the siding by the same method used for stucco house walls. Stucco application is a difficult process with no room for error. Stucco fence construction is best left to a fence or masonry contractor.

Using the same framing techniques, you can apply other masonry facades—tile or thin veneers of stone, brick, or aggregate—to a plywood surface.

Masonry materials are also used for outdoor screens or grilles; these are most commonly built of decorative concrete blocks, but a grillwork screen can also be constructed from flue and drain-tile sections. Several of the more popular screen block designs are shown at right.

Building masonry walls and screens requires specialized masonry techniques beyond the scope of this book. For detailed instructions on masonry wall construction, refer to the *Sunset* books

SCREEN BLOCKS

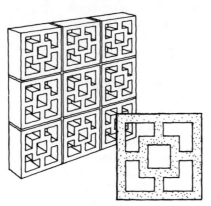

Basic Masonry Illustrated and *How to Build Walks, Walls & Patio Floors.*

Glass

Fences and outdoor screens made of glass can block wind around small patio areas without blocking views or sunlight. (In larger areas, glass, like any solid barrier, is relatively ineffective in blocking wind.) In small areas exposed to the weather, glass is more suitable than plastic panels because of its high resistance to abrasion.

Depending on the effect desired, you can use glass that's clear, translucent (to afford privacy), glare-reducing or tinted (to filter sunlight while allowing a view), or patterned for special effects. Be sure, of course, to use only tempered safety glass—ordinary window glass is too easily broken. In fact, most building codes require tempered safety glass for all outdoor uses. When you buy glass, have the dealer cut it to the size you need.

LUMBER USED IN FENCING

A number of sizes and grades of lumber are suitable for fencing. Most wood fences require 4 by 4 or 6 by 6 posts, and 2 by 4 rails. Lumber used for facing can be pickets, lath, or boards in various sizes, either rough or surfaced.

To extend the life of your fence, you'll want to use lumber that's been pressure-treated with a wood preservative or that is of a decay-resistant type.

Other important considerations in choosing lumber are surface texture, moisture content, actual lumber dimensions, and overall lumber quality.

Decay-resistant lumber

Wood fence members that come in contact with the ground are more susceptible to decay and termite attack than above-ground portions of the fence. Unless lumber is treated with a wood preservative or is cut from the heartwood of a decay-resistant species, it will last only 2 to 3 years underground before becoming structurally unstable.

Pressure-treated lumber. Pressure-treating is a commercial process whereby a preservative is forced deeply into the wood. Fence members treated in this manner will last up to 50 years below ground. Pressure-treated woods have superior decay resistance over woods that have been simply dipped or soaked in a preservative.

Preservatives most commonly used in the pressure-treating process are chromated copper arsenate (CCA) and ammoniacal copper arsenate (ACA), dissolved in water and other solvents.

One drawback to CCA and ACA-treated woods is their color. Both chemicals leave a greenish-brown tinge to the wood. They can, however, be painted or stained over.

Pentachlorophenol and creosote-treated woods are also available but are recommended for industrial or commercial use; the chemicals have unpleasant odors and are toxic to plants.

The American Wood Preservers Bureau (AWPB) has developed a grading system for pressure-treated woods according to the amount of preservative injected into the wood and the depth of its penetration. For residential outdoor use, two levels of treatment are available: woods designated for above-ground use are given the rating LP-2; for below-ground use, LP-22.

To know what you're getting, look for the AWPB grading mark, or the grading mark of an equivalent agency approved by the building code, on each piece of lumber.

Use pressure-treated lumber rated for below ground on all fence members up to 6 inches above ground level. The cut ends of pressure-treated woods should be soaked in a wood preservative, available at home improvement centers.

Decay-resistant species. Some woods have a natural resistance to decay and termite attack. Available species include redwood, red cedar, cypress, and locust. Only the heartwood (darker colored wood toward the tree's center) of these species has this resistance and can be used for fence members in contact with the ground.

"All-heart" lumber will last 5 to 10 years or more underground, depending on soil moisture conditions. Though not as resistant as pressure-treated lumber, this wood may be your choice for reasons of cost, availability, or esthetics.

All-heart lumber is usually more expensive than grades containing both heartwood and the lighter colored sapwood. One way to cut fencing costs is to select posts from the less expensive grades that contain at least 3 feet of solid heartwood at one end, so only the heartwood portion will come in contact with the ground. Remember that the sapwood of the decay-resistant species will not resist decay.

Lumber grades

After lumber is cut from logs, it is sorted and graded according to wood species, quality, moisture content, and eventual use.

To ensure uniform quality from the many independent lumber mills across the country, manufacturers' associations have developed grading standards for each of the commercial wood species. Graded lumber is either identified with a stamp or inventoried by grade before being shipped to the lumberyard.

Generally, lumber grading depends on natural growth characteristics, on defects resulting from milling errors, and on manufacturing techniques in drying and preserving that affect the strength, durability, or appearance of each board.

But these mill-assigned grades only partially indicate the quality of the lumber you're buying. Often, lumberyards and home improvement centers will re-sort and re-designate mill-graded lumber to suit their operations. Redwood, especially, is called whatever the lumber dealer thinks will sell: supreme, deluxe, economy, decking, fence boards, or garden grade.

Unless the pieces are stamped with a grading mark, it's hard to tell which grade you're getting. Also, the quality of lumber differs from one yard to the next, depending on damage from shipping, how the lumber is stacked, and how long it's been sitting there.

So it's important to develop an eye for sound lumber and to hand-select each piece, if possible. Common lumber defects that affect the appearance and strength of wood—and your fence—are shown on the facing page. Learn to spot these defects right at the lumberyard.

Other lumber characteristics

Aside from grading based on natural defects and milling imperfections, lumber is sorted according to surface texture and moisture content.

"Nominal" and "surfaced" sizes. Logs are cut into lumber at the mill, and the dimensions of these different-size boards (the "nominal" sizes) are then used to identify them: a "2 by 4" in its rough state is 2 inches thick by 4 inches wide.

Most lumber is dried, though, and in being dried it shrinks slightly; some of it is then planed for surface quality, which reduces it to a "surfaced" size. So the "2 by 4" you get when ordering dry, surfaced lumber is actually 1½ inches by 3½ inches.

When buying rough lumber, you'll find the actual dimensions will be closer to the nominal ones, depending on the moisture content of the wood and on cutting tolerances allowed by the mill where it's been cut. The chart on the facing page shows the nominal and surfaced sizes of standard lumber. Lath and pickets or boards under 1 inch in thickness or width are identified by their exact size.

Appearance. Whether you use rough or surfaced lumber will depend on how you want your fence to look. Rough or unsurfaced lumber can give the fence a rustic quality (but remember that it's difficult to paint with brush or roller, and it will leave splinters in the hands of any fence climbers).

For a more finished appearance, choose surfaced lumber. It's easier

Standard Dimensions of Surfaced Lumber

| Nominal | | Surfaced Thicknesses & Widths (inches) | |
Thickness (inches)	Width (inches)	Dry	Unseasoned
1	1	$^3/_4$	$^{25}/_{32}$
2	2	$1^1/_2$	$1^9/_{16}$
2	3	$2^1/_2$	$2^9/_{16}$
4	4	$3^1/_2$	$3^9/_{16}$
6	6	$5^1/_2$	$5^5/_8$
6	8	$7^1/_4$	$7^1/_2$
6	10	$9^1/_4$	$9^1/_2$
6	12	$11^1/_4$	$11^1/_2$

to paint or stain, though somewhat more expensive per board foot than rough lumber. To save money, use rough lumber for posts and rails, surfaced lumber for fence siding.

"Unseasoned," "dry," and "kiln-dried." The moisture content of lumber dramatically affects shrinkage, nail holding, and other important properties of wood (the greater its moisture content, the more likely it is to split, warp, or cup as it dries).

Lumber, either air-dried in stacks or kiln-dried, is marked according to its moisture content: S-GRN for "green," unseasoned lumber with moisture content of 20 percent or higher; S-DRY for lumber with a moisture content of 19 percent or less; and MC 15 for lumber dried to 15 percent or less moisture content. "Green" lumber requires further on-site seasoning before use.

Tips on selecting lumber

When you go to choose your lumber, check each board for the defects discussed below. Many lumberyards will allow you to dig through the piles, as long as you keep them neat. The top pieces on the pile are usually the undesirable "flops"—those rejected by other buyers because they are damaged, discolored, or becoming deformed as they dry. So look deeper—wear heavy gloves and bring along a helper when sorting through the pile.

To check for twisting, warping, and cupping (see drawing at right), hold up each board and sight down its length. Boards with long, slow curves are much easier to straighten when nailing than those with tight little crooks.

When selecting lumber for posts and rails, try to avoid "bull's-eye" pieces milled from the center of the log—they tend to crack and warp more than other pieces. Also, select posts and rails with tight, straight-grain patterns, as shown in the drawing below. They are stronger and more decay-resistant than those with wide-grain spacing.

Yes   No   No

Lumber defects. The defects shown at right can affect wood's appearance or strength, or both.

Knots are primarily visual defects, but large, loose ones in posts and rails can weaken a fence. Encased knots—those separated from surrounding wood by a thin layer of bark—are more likely to loosen and fall out than are knots intergrown with surrounding wood (called watertight knots).

Bow and crook are the result of warping due to improper seasoning or stacking—bow is a warp in the wide face of a board, crook a warp in the narrow face. Bow and crook can be avoided by stacking your lumber neatly before use.

Cupping is a warp across a board from edge to edge. Minor cupping can be corrected when the board is nailed.

Wane is the lack of wood at the edge or corner of a board cut from the outside of a log. Posts and rails with this defect may make nailing difficult, causing a weak joint.

Checks and splits are separations of wood fibers caused by improper seasoning or by natural defects in the tree (called *shakes*). Split or badly checked ends should be cut off boards before the boards are used.

Decay is caused by microorganisms that attack moist or wet wood. Treat decayed areas with a water sealer before using lumber.

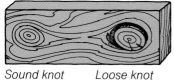

Sound knot   Loose knot

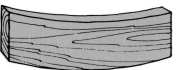

Bow

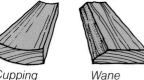

Crook

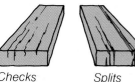

Cupping   Wane

Checks   Splits

Decay

DESIGN IDEAS IN COLOR

Thumb through this colorful gallery for some inspiring examples of fences, garden screens, and gates that work to solve a variety of land-scaping problems. You'll find that many are adaptable to your own yard.

An enduring favorite, the white picket fence here completes a storybook setting with the winding brick walk, lawn, and traditional plantings of ivy and annuals. For details on building a picket fence, see page 66.

FENCING WITH SPLIT RAILS

For a rugged, informal look, split rail fences are economical and easy to construct.

For details on building rail fences, see pages 61–63.

Double post-and-rail *fences are a familiar sight along many country roads. Here, rails are fastened to posts with 5-inch spikes. Boards set across post tops help shed rain.*

When wood was plentiful, *pioneers built zigzag rail fences like this one. Roughhewn notches interlock lapped rails.*

Post-and-rail fence *uses less wood than the rail fences pictured above. Tapered rail ends pass through holes in posts. Rails are 10 feet long.*

POLE FENCES

Readily available, poles can be used just for posts or for the entire fence. Preservative-treated poles offer long life.

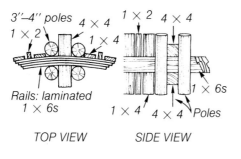

3″–4″ poles
1 × 2
4 × 4
1 × 4

Rails: laminated 1 × 6s

TOP VIEW

1 × 2
4 × 4

1 × 6s

1 × 4
4 × 4
Poles

SIDE VIEW

Gently curving fence threads its way through sets of 8-foot poles. Horizontal 4 by 4s tie poles together; support rails consist of laminated 1 by 6s (see drawing at left). Design: William Louis Kapranos.

Optical illusion: A frame of 4 by 4 posts, with 2 by 4 rails applied in short tangents, is covered with 3-inch-diameter poles nailed to top and sides to create the illusion of a perfect arc. Design: Sherwood Stockwell.

STAKES & PALINGS

Versatile and easy to handle, grapestakes create fences ranging from rustic to formal and require a minimum of maintenance.

For details on building fences with stakes and palings, see page 72.

Formal grapestake fence is painted to high-light foreground plantings; stake tops were trimmed for uniform effect. Design: Nancy Hardesty.

Scaled-down version of the stockade fences encircling frontier forts, this 6-footer has weathered to a pleasing silvery gray. Stockade is one of the more popular styles of prefabricated fencing.

Unlikely combination of wrought iron and rustic stakes creates this attractive entry. Fence rises to match contour of gate top.

PICKET FENCES

For a colonial touch, pickets make a strong boundary fence with an open and airy look; design and cut your own or buy them ready-made.

For details on building picket fences, see page 66.

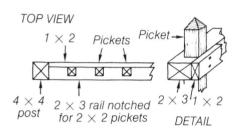

TOP VIEW

1 × 2   Pickets   Picket →

4 × 4 post   2 × 3 rail notched for 2 × 2 pickets   2 × 3 1 × 2   DETAIL

Ivory-colored picket fence jogs back to define front walk clearly. Black finials atop posts and planter beds of marigolds and fibrous begonias further enhance entry. Design: W. David Poot.

Raised planter adds finishing touch to this smart picket enclosing a manicured topiary garden. Drawing above shows how square pickets are inset into rails. Cutting post tops required expertise in finish carpentry. Design: Bill Derringer.

Tall picket is scaled to surrounding pines; natural wood color blends well with foliage. Concrete footing is actually the retainer wall for a sunken tennis court. Design: James B. Pruitt.

Main Street, U.S.A. Its owner designed and built this classic picket with arrow shaped tops, but left the tedium of cutting picket and post tops to a cabinet shop.

BOARD FENCES

For strength and privacy, board fences are hard to beat. They're easy to construct—in an almost unlimited variety of designs—but can be costly.

For details on building board fences, see page 68.

Understated beauty: The simplicity of this sawtooth board fence focuses attention on the textures, patterns, and colors of the boards themselves. Design: Ken Slusser.

Staggered sections of diagonal board fencing act as a windbreak and offer privacy to an expansive lawn area. Design: Ken Slusser.

Espaliered shrubs and contrasting posts and rails break the monotony of this long streetside fence. Boards are resawn 1 by 6s.

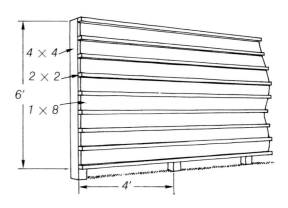

Rustic beauty of natural wood carries over from house to horizontal board fence. Drawing above shows siding detail. Design: Robert Price.

. . . Board fences

Where the fence of boards must end, pergola created in wood makes the point. Design: Gene Kunit.

Louver fence defines yard area, yet allows view of woods beyond. Louvers block view of yard from public trail outside. For details on building louver fences, see page 70. Design: Gene Kunit.

FENCES OF SOLID PANELS

Panels of plywood or hardboard can be surfaced with other materials for a wide variety of patterns and textures.

For details on building panel fences, see page 74.

Stucco over plywood panels *gives a solid look to this fence, while open sections allow air to flow through patio.*

Plywood panels *set into a sturdy frame shelter city lot from street noises and curious passers-by. White makes a good backdrop for roses. Design: Richard Schadt.*

Disappearing act: *Continuity with the wood shake fence camouflages this entry gate; the only giveaways are brass address numbers and mail slot. Design: Paul Petroelje and Tom Gerlach.*

LATTICE FENCES & GARDEN SCREENS

Lattice fences and screens can be plain or fancy, of heavy or light lumber; they're excellent for climbing plants.

For details on building lattice fences, see page 77.

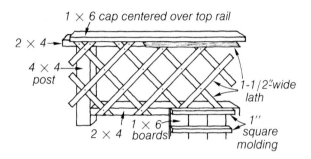

1 × 6 cap centered over top rail

2 × 4

4 × 4 post

1-1/2"-wide lath

1 × 6 boards

2 × 4

1" square molding

Cool retreat: *Fence top repeats latticework on gazebo roof, and solid white fence defines plantings. Drawing above shows fence top detail. Design: Richard Murray.*

Heavy-duty lattice fence *uses 2 by 2s for lattice-work. The window was an alternative to spoiling the shape of a mature white oak. Design: Richard Schadt.*

Lattice artwork gives Victorian style to this 8-foot screen. Its height discourages intruders; open design lends a spacious feeling to a small city lot.

Finish moldings on posts and rails recall the attention to detail in lattice fences of the late 19th century. This fence and gate were recent additions. Design: Tom Leonard.

FENCES OF ORNAMENTAL METAL

Sturdy and classic, ornamental metal fences are at home between posts of metal, masonry, or wood; most are custom designs.

Relic from the past: This venerable antique has withstood many seasons. The design can be reproduced by a metal worker (see page 14).

Low ornamental fence and gate are not wrought iron, but lighter-weight tubular steel. Prefabricated fence sections are spot-welded together on site.

Perfect pool fence: *Tall, virtually unclimbable open metalwork allows clear view of young swimmers' antics from outer yard. Prefabricated sections are 6 feet tall, the minimum required for pool fences in some communities.*

Not all ornamental fencing *must be black. Here, low prefab sections are fastened to wood posts with lag bolts—a do-it-yourself project. Easy way to paint sections is to use rust-resistant paint in spray cans.*

THE LOW ONES

To outline your property, control foot traffic, or accent the landscape, a low fence may be all you need.

Low post-and-rail fence uses less lumber than most wood fences; 2 by 6 rails are mortised into 4 by 4 posts.

Extending entry handrail, fence posts and uprights are fastened to raised wood walk; chambered 4 by 12 curb follows driveway contour.

Simplicity itself: Low chain fence is just enough to discourage short-cutting through plants. Countersunk bolts attach chain ends to corner posts.

Housewrecker was source of antique railing and posts used in this fence. For similar finds, look in the Yellow Pages under "Demolition Contractors."

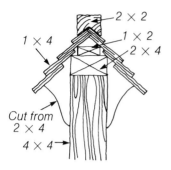

2×2

1×4

1×2

2×4

Cut from 2×4

4×4

Japanese sleeve fence completes oriental-style garden. Top detail shown in drawing above. Design: Toshio Saburomaru and Bill Comstock.

HILLSIDE FENCES

There are several ways to climb a hillside; step up with panels, extend the fence to fit the slope, or follow the contour of the hill.

Flowing gracefully down a steep hillside lot, fence of narrow grapestakes easily follows contour of the land. Design: Gene Kunit.

Step-down board and lattice fence and gate protect city yard on a busy hillside street. Brick footing fills gaps at bottom. Design: James McLean.

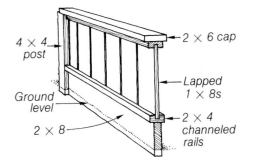

4 × 4 post
2 × 6 cap
Lapped 1 × 8s
Ground level
2 × 8
2 × 4 channeled rails

Slight change in terrain? This low fence manages easily: top remains level while bottom dips to cross swale. Drawing above shows fence detail.

Brick columns march uniformly down the hill; boards between are cut along bottom to follow slope. Design: Roy Rydell.

Clean lines mark this shingle fence set atop a concrete footing; upper edge steps down one course of shingles every 6 feet.

Wood and wire fence can easily navigate a slope, provided top and bottom rails remain parallel. Design: Ken Slusser.

FENCES THAT
MIRROR THE HOUSE

Make the fence an extension of the house by using the siding of the house on the fence as well.

Siding for house carries over to low front-yard fence. Fence top reflects window design, and colors tie fence and house together. Design: Roy Rydell.

Graceful integration of house, fence, and tree show an eye for the esthetic. Design: Lloyd Tupper.

Extension of the house: Low front-yard fence creates a formal courtyard. Trellis over windows will offer privacy when vines mature. Design: Jack Stafford.

OUTDOOR SCREENS

Use garden screens to block the wind, divide the garden, add privacy, or hide a work area.

For details on building garden screens, see page 79.

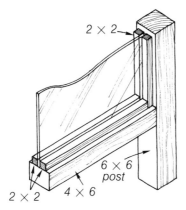

Glass wind screen *shelters hillside patio area while allowing panoramic view of hills beyond. Screen was designed for standard-size glass door panels (see drawing at left). Design: Ortha Zebroski.*

Poolside screening *shelters house from sunlight and pool glare, yet allows those inside to keep an eye on young swimmers. Design: Roy Rydell.*

Short screen *defines side entry to yard and creates backdrop for carefully tended plantings.*

Notched 1 by 2s *add an extra dimension to an otherwise ordinary lattice screen. If cutting notches seems tedious, have a cabinetmaker do the work. Design: Roy Rydell.*

Louver screen *attached to poolhouse gives swimmers both privacy and shelter from the wind. For details on building louver screens, see page 70. Design: Gene Kunit.*

OUTDOOR ROOMS

Extend your living space—create outdoor rooms by combining fences with garden screens.

Bilevel deck is made cozy by tall screen. Translucent fiberglass panels afford privacy, but admit filtered sunlight for potted plants. Design: Roy Rydell.

Rooftop garden room comes complete with large picture window in lattice screen so owners may enjoy lofty view of world outside. Design: Roy Rydell.

No hot tub *is complete without privacy. Lath screen and carefully arranged tall plantings obscure visions from outside without giving bathers a boxed-in feeling. Design: Don Boos.*

Room for plants: *Unique garden structure offers shade for prized plantings on deck. Seating at left is backed by wood and wire fence surrounding deck. Design: Richard Schadt.*

FENCES & SCREENS THAT GROW

Climbing plants do well against a fence; wire, lattice, grapestake, and split rail fences are favorite backgrounds.

Living sculpture: *Formal espalier is displayed against horizontal 2 by 6s nailed to plywood and lattice screen. The basics of espaliering shrubs are discussed on page 87.*

Living fence: *2 by 4-inch wire mesh on wood frame provides the support for ivy "siding." Ivy must be trimmed frequently to maintain desired effect. For details on building wood and wire fences, see page 76. Design: Bill Derringer.*

Carefully trained ivy adorns this 6-foot grapestake fence. Maintenance takes time, but the results are striking. Design: Jack Stafford.

Pink roses contrast with weathered gray post-and-rail fence separating expansive lawn from street. Tapered rails are mortised into holes cut in posts.

Climbing grape helps break up the dizzying lines of this long lattice screen—and yields fruit in autumn. Screen offers privacy and shelter from hot afternoon sun.

Fence Plantings **43**

GATES: FROM SIMPLE TO ORNATE

The garden gate can be more than a section of fence on hinges; let it invite your guests and reflect your personality.

For details on building gates, see page 88.

Dutch gate may be opened as a whole unit or—with a flick of a bolt—at the top only. Design: Richard Murray.

Oriental-style gate looks sturdy enough to protect a temple from samurai attacks. Hinges are custom-made; top latch is standard hardware item.

Sturdy pergola, brick posts help scale this low fence and gate to a large, two-story house. Uprights are 2 by 2s; gate frame is made of 2 by 4s mitered at corners. Design: Mary Gordon.

A cool entry: Delicate vines adorn rustic gate and pergola. All gate hardware is standard, including cane bolt at bottom that keeps gate locked from inside.

Roof-style pergola *affords visitors temporary shelter from rain or hot sun. Brick posts and shingled pergola reflect house roof, chimney, and brick siding in background. Design: Roy Rydell.*

Profusion of morning glory *crowns front entry gate and pergola. Sturdy 6 by 6 gate posts support vines. Decorative inset for gate came from a large import store.*

Large caster *supports the weight of this heavy wood driveway gate. Wisteria at left will eventually be trained over beam above gate.*

Work of art: Cypress trees on the property provided the subject for the copper plated inset on this driveway gate. Sliding gate is operated electrically. Design: Richard Murray.

Light for their size: Lattice-work reduces the weight of large driveway gates. Small casters assist in opening and prevent gate from sagging.

Visitors must stop to admire the craftsmanship of these double entry gates before passing through. Plywood insets were cut out with a portable jigsaw and beveled with a router. Design: James L. Aldrich.

BUILDING BASICS

- *Estimating and ordering fence materials*
- *Plotting the fence*
- *Installing posts*
- *Adding rails and siding*
- *Paints and stains—the finishing touches*

Once your fence plans are complete, it's time to take them off the drafting board (or dining room table) and put them into action. The first step will be to determine quantities of materials you'll need and order them. Next, you'll be taking your plans outside to begin construction.

Fence building can be divided into three stages: the relatively easy, preliminary stage of plotting the fence (locating and marking where posts will go); the somewhat more difficult stage of installing posts (digging holes, setting and aligning posts); and the third stage of adding the rails and siding.

Each of these stages consists of a number of specific steps. The actual sequence of steps will vary with the type of fence you build and with other factors such as fence length and surrounding landscape conditions. Some builders, for instance, like to set all posts in place, and then attach rails and siding. This is the easiest procedure for fences that have their posts set in concrete (see page 54).

Another method involves assembling the fence in sections, filling in the rails and siding whenever two posts are in place. This method is used for many prefabricated fences and for those fences where sections are built on the ground, then lifted into place. If posts and rails are fitted together with interlocking joints, the rails must be attached before the posts are set.

No matter what sequence of steps you follow, you'll find helpful the basic fence building methods outlined in this chapter. You can tailor the procedures to fit your specific situation.

ESTIMATING AND ORDERING FENCE MATERIALS

You'll save time and money if you make accurate calculations of all materials needed to build your fence, and then purchase all your materials at once.

Rough estimates made early in your planning will help you to compare overall costs of various fence designs, but more detailed estimates are needed for ordering materials. You'll base your final calculations on your completed scale drawings of your fence (page 10). The following sections will help you estimate quantities.

If you're building a gate into the fence, be sure to include all necessary gate materials in your order. (For planning and building gates, see pages 88–95.)

If you've chosen one of the fence or screen designs on pages 61–79, use the drawings and materials listed there to help in your figuring.

How much lumber?

Estimating lumber for a fence or an outdoor screen is primarily a matter of measuring and counting up the number of pieces needed for construction.

The most economical fence designs use standard lumber lengths, which keep cutting and waste to a minimum. But if your design requires odd-size pieces, determine the most economical way to cut them from available lumber lengths (lumber is sold in multiples of 2 feet). For instance, if you need $4\frac{1}{2}$-foot boards, you can cut four of them from an 18-footer with no waste, rather than cutting them from a 6, 10, or 14-footer with unusable short pieces left over.

You can reduce your lumber costs even further by ordering the most readily available, suitable species and the lowest grade of lumber for your needs. You'll find it easier to make intelligent choices by looking at the lumber that is available in local lumberyards.

First, count the number of posts in your plan and determine their lengths. The post length includes the post height (above ground) and the post depth (below ground). To determine how deep posts should be set, see page 53.

Next, determine the total amount of material needed for rails and siding. Using your elevation drawing as a guide (page 10), determine the number and lengths of pieces needed to build one section of fence; then multiply this amount by the number of sections in your fence. If sections are of unequal lengths, rails and siding will have to be figured separately for each section.

Finally, add 10 percent to the total number of rails, and siding materials, to allow for waste and building errors.

Figuring out hardware

Before ordering your lumber, estimate the amount of nails and other hardware you'll be using. Most lumberyards and building suppliers either carry or can order most everything you'll need, so having a complete materials list on hand will save you extra trips.

Because you'll use nails by the hundreds in all but the smallest of fence projects, you'll want to have the right nails on hand. Figure out first the types and sizes of nails your fence will require, then the quantities you'll need (nails are generally sold by the pound).

All nails used in fencing should be corrosion resistant. Top-quality galvanized nails are preferred for most fence projects, because they are unlikely to corrode in wet conditions or to lose their holding power over a long period of time. Stainless steel or aluminum nails are also effective but are more expensive than galvanized nails.

The nails most often used in fencing are "common" nails and "box" nails, which differ only in diameter. The larger diameter of common nails gives them more holding power than box nails, but "commons" require more muscle to drive and are more likely to split the wood.

Finishing nails are best used for decorative trims, moldings, or fence details, because their small heads are relatively invisible. But their holding power is considerably less than that of common or box nails.

Besides diameter and corrosion-resistance, nail length also affects holding power: use nails that are three times as long as the thickness of the board they're expected to hold.

The chart on the next page gives penny size (the standard nail measurement abbreviated as "d"), length, diameter and number per pound for common, box, and finishing nails.

To compute the quantity you need, count up the number of each size and type of nail required for one section of fence, and then multiply by the total number of fence sections. Using the chart, translate the number into pounds; then add 10 percent to the total figure for each nail type required.

Fasteners other than nails (bolts, screws, brackets, or staples) are estimated in a similar manner (number needed per section times number of sections plus 10 percent). All fasteners and metal hardware should be corrosion resistant.

Estimating concrete and gravel

Standard fence construction requires that posts be set in concrete (see page 54), though lighter fences—such as most post and board or low picket fences—may have their posts set in earth-and-gravel fill (see page 54).

The amount of concrete or gravel needed will depend on the number and size of post holes, and how much of each hole will be filled by the post itself. Estimating accurately isn't easy.

Generally speaking, if you're setting 4-inch-diameter posts in concrete, you'll need $\frac{1}{3}$ cubic foot of gravel in the bottom of each hole and $\frac{2}{3}$ cubic foot of concrete. When setting posts in earth-and-gravel fill, you'll need $\frac{1}{3}$ cubic foot of gravel for the bottom of the hole and 1 cubic foot to mix with the earth.

Unless you're fencing several acres, buying concrete ready-mixed in sacks (sand, gravel, cement—you add the water) is the

Common

Box

Finishing

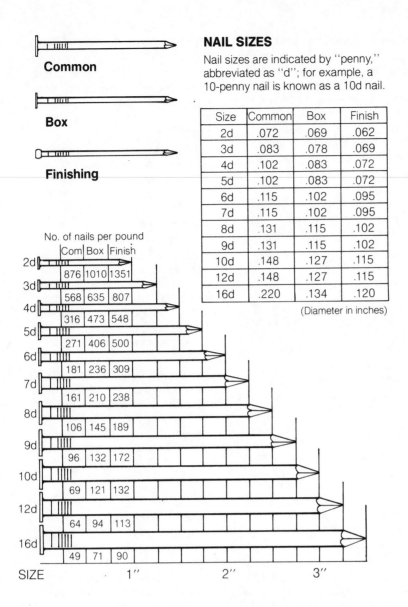

NAIL SIZES

Nail sizes are indicated by "penny," abbreviated as "d"; for example, a 10-penny nail is known as a 10d nail.

Size	Common	Box	Finish
2d	.072	.069	.062
3d	.083	.078	.069
4d	.102	.083	.072
5d	.102	.083	.072
6d	.115	.102	.095
7d	.115	.102	.095
8d	.131	.115	.102
9d	.131	.115	.102
10d	.148	.127	.115
12d	.148	.127	.115
16d	.220	.134	.120

(Diameter in inches)

No. of nails per pound

Size	Com	Box	Finish
2d	876	1010	1351
3d	568	635	807
4d	316	473	548
5d	271	406	500
6d	181	236	309
7d	161	210	238
8d	106	145	189
9d	96	132	172
10d	69	121	132
12d	64	94	113
16d	49	71	90

SIZE 1" 2" 3"

most convenient in terms of ordering and then mixing on the job. And it just happens that a 90-pound sack of ready-mixed concrete makes about ⅔ cubic foot, so you can figure one bag for each post and hole.

You can buy gravel from garden centers, quarries, or building suppliers in almost any amount by the sack or by the truckload. Ask for it by the cubic foot or cubic yard (27 cubic feet equals 1 cubic yard).

How much paint or stain?

To figure the amount of paint or stain you'll need, calculate the total number of square feet of fence surface to be covered; then check the product's label for the manufacturer's estimate of coverage (number of square feet per gallon).

If your fence or screen has a fairly solid, unbroken surface (panels, butted boards, louvers), simply multiply fence height by overall length; add 10 percent to the figure to be sure you buy enough for the job. Double the amount if you plan to paint both sides.

If the fence has an open design (post and board, spaced lath, or pickets), estimate the square feet of board surface in each section; then multiply by the number of sections.

Add 10 percent to the total. On all estimates, double the total if you're going to apply a second coat.

Buying materials

Once your materials list is complete, you're ready to order.

If possible, hand-pick all lumber from your building supplier or lumberyard. Or if your fence project is very large, you may prefer to place an order through a lumberyard and have the lumber delivered.

In either case, visit several suppliers to compare prices and inspect lumber quality before you buy (see page 17 for tips on shopping for lumber). Take along your materials list and get competitive bids on the total amount of lumber and other materials you'll be buying. If you simply order by phone and have the lumber delivered sight unseen, you may be buying a pig in a poke.

Remember that you'll save time and money if you order as many materials (lumber, nails, concrete, paint, and hardware) as possible at a single time from one supplier.

Storing lumber. When you get your lumber home, stack it neatly, with some weight like bricks along the top to prevent warping, and cover with polyethylene to keep it dry. You can ruin a pile of new wood if you let it sit outside for even a day in the rain or very hot sun.

If you bought green or wet lumber, let it dry for a few weeks by stacking it evenly in the shade to allow uniform drying (the garage is a good place if there's room). Place spacer strips between layers so air can circulate and help dry the wood.

PLOTTING THE FENCE

The first step in building your fence or screen is to locate the exact course it will take and mark the line with stakes and string.

If you're building the fence on or next to a boundary or property line, you must be certain of the exact location of that line.

Of course, if the original survey stakes or markers are still marking the boundaries of your newly surveyed lot, you're fairly safe in using them for the fence line. Also, if the description of your property is exact enough in your deed, you might be able to measure the lines yourself.

But if you're not absolutely positive where the line is, have a surveyor or civil engineer lay out the corner stakes of your property. Though such a survey will cost you a fee, it will cost much less than moving the fence later.

If you're replacing an existing boundary or division fence, don't assume that the original one was built exactly on the line. In all cases, check the survey and your neighbors to avoid any possible misunderstanding.

If, after checking all sources of information, you still have doubts about the boundary locations, you may want to set the posts inside the line just to be safe. (For discussion of the legal aspects of boundary fencing, see page 8.)

If you're not building a boundary fence—if your fence or screen will lie within your property—simply measure the desired length of fence line and mark the location of end and corner posts. Tips for marking off right angles, curves, and hillside fences can be found below.

Tools. To establish the fence line, you'll need a 50-foot or 100-foot steel tape measure; a ball of mason's twine or any nonstretchable, tightly twisted nylon string, such as braided fishing line; some stakes (available ready-cut at lumberyards); a hammer (to drive the stakes); some large box nails; a few scraps of paper; and a piece of colored chalk. To transfer post locations from the twine to the ground, you'll need a plumb line (usually available at hardware stores or from building material suppliers).

Plotting a straight fence

Here's how you plot a straight line for a fence:

1. Mark end or corner post locations with a solidly driven stake.

2. Run mason's twine or string between stakes, drawing it tight and tying it firmly to stakes. If bushes or other low obstructions are in the way, use tall stakes so twine will clear them. If fence line is very long, you may have to prop up twine with intermediate stakes every 100 feet or so to prevent twine from sagging. Add stakes carefully, keeping twine in alignment.

3. Locate sites for remaining posts by measuring along twine and marking post centers on twine with chalk.

4. Use large nails stuck through scraps of paper to mark spots on ground directly below marks on twine. If twine is suspended a foot or more above ground, use a plumb line to transfer marks; otherwise simply depress string to ground (see drawing below).

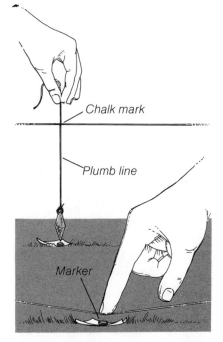

Chalk mark

Plumb line

Marker

Plotting a right angle

If your fence layout calls for corners that form an exact 90° angle, use the 3–4–5 measuring method described below. (Builders commonly use this method to lay out building foundations):

1. Establish first fence line (point A to point B), following directions above.

2. Establish second fence line (point B to point C) roughly perpendicular to first, substituting a batterboard for end stake beyond point C as shown below.

3. On first fence line, measure and then chalk-mark twine 4 feet from corner stake B, then mark second fence line 3 feet from corner stake B.

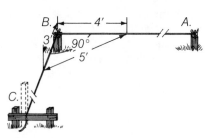

4. Adjust second fence line on batterboard until diagonal measurement between the two marks equals 5 feet—the two lines will then form a 90° angle—and mark a spot on ground directly beneath point where string is tied to batterboard. *Caution:* Because string stretches when pulled, each time you adjust the second fence line you should check the location of the 3-foot mark before measuring the diagonal.

5. Remove batterboard and retie twine to a stake driven at marked location (point C), being careful not to move twine out of alignment.

6. Locate remaining posts as described in steps 3 and 4 of ''Plotting a straight line fence'' (above).

Plotting a curve

You don't have to be a mathematician to plot a symmetrical curve in your fence line. All you'll need, along with the plotting tools and materials listed above, is a very large compass for scribing your arc in the dirt.

The compass you'll be making is one of the earliest tools known to mankind—all you need is a strong, smooth-surfaced rod, pipe, or dowel about 3 feet long for a pivot point, a length of heavy cord or rope (window sash cord, cotton rope, or clothesline works well), and a straight, pointed stick.

Plot the curve according to the steps below:

1. Stretch twine between end stakes of intended curve as shown in the drawing below.

2. Measure exactly halfway between the two end stakes and drive a stake to mark this location.

3. From center stake, run a second line exactly 90° to the first, using steps just described in "Plotting a right angle." Length of second line should be roughly equal to that of first.

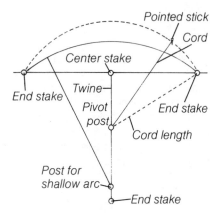

4. Drive 3-foot rod, pipe, or dowel at a chosen pivot point along line perpendicular to fence line. The farther away from fence line you drive the pivot post, the shallower the arc will be—you may have to try several positions before you get desired arc.

5. Measure cord to reach from pivot post to one of the end posts. Then attach one end of cord to pipe, other end to pointed stick.

6. Keeping line taut, scribe an arc in ground from one end post to the other.

7. To locate intermediate posts, bend a flexible steel or cloth tape measure around arc and mark desired post spacing.

For tips on building a curved fence, see page 11.

Plotting hillside fencing

If you've planned a fence for a hillside with a very steep or irregular slope, it's best to have a professional lay out and build the fence. But if the slope is fairly gradual and uniform (no humps or depressions along the fence line), you can plot it yourself, using one of the methods described below.

Contour fencing. To plot contour fencing (fencing that follows the slope), drive stakes at end post locations and stretch twine between them as shown in drawing A below. The twine should be high enough to clear the ground between the stakes. For rolling or uneven terrain, you may have to use intermediate stakes to keep the twine at an even height above the ground.

Measure and mark with chalk the intermediate post locations on the string—then, using your plumb line, transfer marks to the ground beneath, as shown in the drawing below and on page 51. Use nails stuck through pieces of paper for ground markers.

Stepped fencing. Drive a stake at the uphill end of the fence line and attach twine to it at ground level. At the downhill end, drive a stake tall enough to allow leveling of the twine, once it's stretched between the stakes (drawing B below) Then level the twine, using a 2-foot level.

Measure and mark intermediate post locations along the twine and transfer marks to the ground with a plumb line, as shown below and the drawing on page 51.

When you're ready to install the posts, remove the stakes and twine, and dig the post holes. Then, if you're setting 4 by 4-inch posts, relocate the stakes 2 inches to one side of their original position; con-

PLOTTING HILLSIDE FENCING

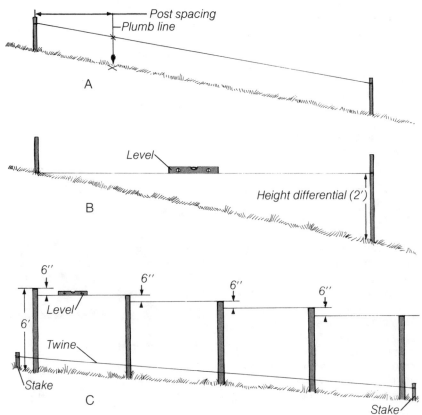

nect the twine parallel to the slope; and use the twine as a guide to align the posts as you set them. For complete instructions on installing posts, see below.

If you want the fence to step evenly down the hill—like a flight of stairs—use the following method to determine the height of each section (dimensions are given here only as an example):

1. Follow directions above for creating a level with twine (drawing B on facing page); then measure distance from twine to ground at downhill end stake to get height differential of slope (2 feet).

2. Divide height differential by the number of sections in fence (2 feet divided by 4 sections). Resulting measurement will be amount of drop for each section (6 inches, as shown in drawing C on facing page).

3. Once post holes are dug and twine reconnected parallel to slope, as described above, set post on uphill end of fence to desired height (6 feet); then measure amount of drop (6 inches) from top of post and mark it on side facing where next post will be set.

4. Set next post loosely in hole and stretch a piece of twine from mark on first post to top of second. Using a 2-foot level, adjust height of second post until twine is level. Continue this process with successive posts down fence line until all posts are set.

INSTALLING POSTS

Post installation—setting and aligning posts—is the most important part of fence building. If posts are not set firmly in the ground, they'll become the Achilles' heel of an otherwise solidly built fence. They must be aligned vertically ("plumb") in their holes and located exactly on the line or you'll encounter difficulties when adding rails and siding materials.

The process of installing posts can be divided into three steps: (1) digging post holes; (2) setting posts; and (3) aligning posts. Steps 2 and 3 are in fact a simultaneous process, best done by two people— one to hold and align the post while the other fills the hole with concrete or earth and gravel.

There are a number of ways in which fence builders install posts; the most commonly accepted methods are described and illustrated here. If posts are to be cut (dadoed or mortised) to accept rails (page 57), be sure to do this before the posts are set.

Digging post holes

The size of the post hole you dig depends upon the height and weight of your fence, the stresses it must withstand, and the soil conditions along the fence line.

The tools you use to dig the holes will depend on the number of post holes and the type of soil. If the ground is very hard to work, or you've planned very many post holes, you may want to rent power digging tools or hire someone to do the digging.

What size? Most residential fencing between 3 and 6 feet tall calls for posts set a minimum of 2 feet deep. Posts are commonly available in 6, 7, and 8-foot lengths for 4, 5, and 6-foot fences, respectively. End posts and gate posts need more support and are generally set 1 foot deeper than line posts. They should therefore be 1 foot longer than line posts to begin with.

Fences and screens that may call for posts set deeper than 2 feet are those over 6 feet in height; those subjected to unusual stresses (high winds, unstable soil, or heavy siding materials); those used to contain large animals; and those subject to frost heaving (discussed on page 54).

A good rule to follow in these situations is to sink posts at least one third their total length into the ground and then set them in concrete.

The bottom of the post hole should be slightly wider than the

top to provide a solid base. To allow water to drain past the bottom of the posts, dig the hole 4 to 6 inches deeper than the posts will be set and fill the bottom with rocks and gravel.

The hole diameter should be 2½ to 3 times the width of square posts or the diameter of round ones (10 to 12 inches for 4-inch-thick posts). Local fence contractors may be willing to advise you on soil conditions that affect fence building in your area and offer suggestions for setting posts.

Digging tools. For small digging jobs (up to a dozen post holes), you'll probably want to use hand tools and muscle. The two most popular hand tools for digging are the auger and the two-handled clamshell digger (see drawing below). Both augers and clamshell diggers are available from tool rental shops.

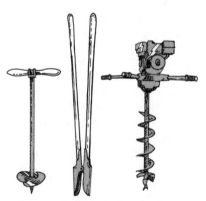

Auger   Clamshell   Power digger (earth drill)

The auger works best in loose earth. Though the clamshell is best in harder soil, it's difficult to use for digging a hole deeper than 3 feet, because the side walls of the hole interfere with the spreading of the handles. Also, working the handles tends to break down the walls, producing a wider, rougher hole than necessary.

In rocky soil, you may also rely on a heavy bar or a jack hammer to break the rocks.

Power diggers (also called earth drills) will save you time and energy on larger jobs. Models that can be operated by one or two persons are available at most tool rental shops (see drawing on previous page). When using a power digger, you may also need a clamshell digger or small garden spade to remove loose dirt from the hole.

Setting posts

To ensure a strong installation, most fence posts are set in concrete, though some may be set in earth-and-gravel fill. If the soil is stable (not subject to sliding, cracking, or frost heaving), earth-and-gravel fill is a perfectly adequate setting material for lightweight fences—such as post and board, lath, or picket—or for fences 4 feet or less in height.

The two methods are described below.

Setting posts in concrete. If your fence design calls for rails recessed into posts by means of a notch, dado, or mortise, these should be cut into the posts before the posts are set. For instructions on cutting these joints, see page 57. Using dry ready-mixed concrete (cement, sand, and gravel all in one bag) is preferable for most fence or screen installations.

If you're mixing your own concrete, though, use a mix of 2 parts (by volume) cement, 3 parts sand, and 5 parts gravel. When you add the water, keep the mix rather stiff (dry) to avoid having dirt from the hole infiltrate the concrete, and to keep the post in alignment.

Begin by placing a large stone in the bottom of each post hole; this will keep the post from sinking once set (see drawing above right). To set the post, first pour 4 to 6 inches of gravel (and rocks, if you have them) into the hole. Next, place the post in the hole and shovel in an additional 4 inches of gravel. This will keep the concrete from getting under the post and trapping water that will speed decay.

Finally, shovel in the concrete evenly around the post. As you fill, tamp it with a broomstick or

SETTING POSTS

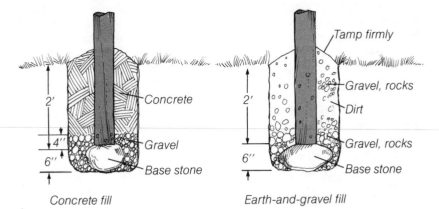

Concrete fill

Earth-and-gravel fill

a capped end of a steel pipe, to work out any air pockets in the mix. Check and adjust post for alignment.

To extend the mix, keep a supply of washed rocks on hand, and place them around the perimeter of the hole as you pour. The concrete should be poured 1 or 2 inches above ground level and sloped *away* from the post to divert water, as shown in the drawing above.

Posts freshly set in concrete can be forced into alignment and plumb for perhaps 20 minutes after the pour; they should then be left alone for 2 days before rails and siding are nailed on.

Setting posts in earth-and-gravel fill. Vigorous tamping is the key to a successful installation using earth-and-gravel fill.

First, place a big stone in each post hole and surround with 4 to 6 inches of rocks or gravel (drawing above). Tamp well, using a good length of 2 by 4 lumber. Place the post in the hole, and shovel in gravel a little at a time while you align the post and plumb it with a level. Continue filling with earth and gravel, tamping firmly after every 2 or 3 inches.

If the hole is wide, big rocks jammed around the post near the surface will minimize side movement. Slope the top of the fill so that water will run away from the post. In light, sandy soil—which offers easy shoveling but poor stability for fence posts—nail 1 by 4 cleats of heartwood cedar or red-

wood, or pressure-treated wood across the fence posts near ground level (see drawing below).

Frost heaving. Frozen ground in winter brings two problems: frost heaving (the shifting of ground caused by alternate freezing and thawing of the soil) and concrete cracking. To minimize damage from heaving, dig post holes down to a foot below normal frost line; shovel in several inches of gravel; drive nails part way into the sides of each post near its bottom end, and place this end in gravel; pour concrete around nail area; add gravel to a depth of 6 inches below ground level, then complete the fill with concrete.

To prevent concrete collars from cracking when posts contract and and expand from extreme temperature changes, cut shingles to width of posts, oil them, and place alongside each post before you pour. When concrete has set, remove the shingles and fill the open spaces with tar or sand.

Aligning posts

The most critical step in post installation is aligning the posts so that they are exactly vertical and in a straight line. Remember it's much easier to set and align posts if you have a helper.

Tools you'll need include mason's twine, hammer, 2-foot level, a short length of 1 by 2 lumber from which to cut spacer blocks, and a few 4-penny nails.

Corner post method. This method works best for relatively short sections of fence or screen (100 feet or less). Begin with two corner or end posts; position them with their faces parallel, then plumb with a level, as shown in the drawing below, and set them permanently.

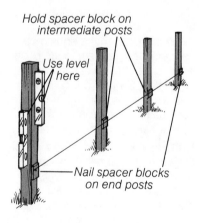

Hold spacer block on intermediate posts

Use level here

Nail spacer blocks on end posts

Next, tack 1 by 2 spacer blocks (about 2 inches long) to the end posts, about 2 feet above ground level. Stretch twine between the two end posts, attaching it to the spacer blocks as shown above. The purpose of the blocks is to keep intermediate posts from touching the string and throwing it out of alignment.

Set and align intermediate posts at a distance away from the string

that is exactly equal to the thickness of the spacer block, by holding a spare block against each post to measure distance. Plumb posts on two adjacent faces as you go.

Fill holes carefully, checking to see that each post remains vertical as you work.

Once all posts are in, make a final check by eye to be sure posts have remained in alignment. Keep in mind that posts set in concrete can be adjusted for up to 20 minutes after the concrete is poured; after that they should not be moved.

Aligning and setting posts successively. For very long sections of fence, such as country fencing, the corner post method may be impractical because the twine stretched between end posts will sag. One way to solve this problem is to build the fence in sections, using the corner post method for about every 100 feet.

Or you can set and align posts successively—one after the other—until you reach the end of the fence line. This method should be used when building a mortised post-and-rail fence (see pages 62–63). Simply move the stakes used for plotting the fence 2 inches to one side of the post centers, reconnect the twine, and line the posts up, using the twine as a guide. Use a level on adjacent faces of the post to align them vertically, as shown in the drawing at left. Be careful that in setting posts you do not move the twine out of alignment.

Aligning and setting posts by yourself. You can set posts without a helper if you use braces as an extra pair of hands to hold the posts; then align posts, using either of the methods just described, and set them in concrete or earth-and-gravel fill.

Make the braces from 6-foot lengths of 1 by 4s and stakes, shown in the drawing above. To position them, drive stakes into the ground and attach the braces so they can be lifted and nailed to adjacent sides of the fence post as shown. Use only one nail to attach each brace to the stake, so the

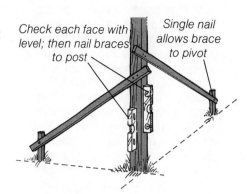

Check each face with level; then nail braces to post

Single nail allows brace to pivot

brace pivots freely.

If you're using concrete fill, make enough braces to hold four posts (eight braces total) so you can set additional posts while the concrete hardens around the first post.

For earth-and-gravel fill: Place base stone and 6 inches of rocks or gravel in bottom of hole. Position the post in the hole, and hold it roughly vertical while you shovel in enough earth and gravel so the post will stand by itself but can still be adjusted. Position the braces as described above. Before attaching the braces to the post, use a level on adjacent post faces to align the post vertically as shown in the drawing above.

Being careful not to move the post out of alignment, attach braces to the post—tack nails so they can be easily removed later. Fill the remainder of the hole with earth and gravel, following directions on facing page. As you work, frequently check post alignment with your level and readjust braces if necessary. When the post is firmly set, carefully remove the braces and use them on the next post.

For concrete fill: First, position the braces as described above. Put a base stone and 6 inches of gravel into the hole, place the post in, and, holding the post roughly vertical, lift the support arms and attach them to the post. Tack nails so they can be easily removed later. Fill the hole with concrete as described on facing page.

Immediately after concrete is poured, carefully remove the support arms from the post, align the post vertically with a 2-foot level, then reattach the arms, being careful not to remove the aligned post. Allow the concrete to set for at least 1 hour before removing the braces. Meanwhile, use the three additional sets of braces you made to install successive posts. By the time the fourth post is set, the braces on the first can be removed and used on the fifth, and so forth.

Adjusting posts for height. Many fence designs call for posts set at precisely the same height so that their tops are level with each other. Examples include fences with rails attached to the top of the posts, and fences with rails recessed into posts by means of a notch or dado (see next page). Adjust posts for height at the same time you align them—you'll need a helper. Here are two methods:

If you're using the corner post method of alignment (page 55) and the overall fence length is 50 feet or less, adjust the post height as follows (see drawing below):

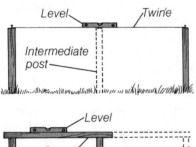

1. Set one end post to desired height, and place other end post loosely in its hole.

2. Stretch twine tightly across tops of end posts and level the twine (using a 2-foot level) by adjusting loose post up or down in its hole.

3. When twine is level, set loose post firmly in place.

4. Set intermediate posts so their tops are even with twine—make

sure you don't throw string out of alignment by setting posts too high.

If you're setting posts successively (page 55) or if fence will be over 50 feet long, use the following method (see drawing above):

1. Set first post to desired height; then place the next post in line loosely in its hole.

2. Lay a straight piece of 2 by 4 across tops of two posts (first check 2 by 4 to make sure it's not warped).

3. Center a 2-foot level on top of 2 by 4 and hold in position, checking for level while your helper adjusts and sets the next post.

Continue this method for each post in line.

ADDING RAILS AND SIDING

Once the fence posts are set and aligned, the hardest part of your fence building is over. The next step is to carefully attach the rails and siding (boards, pickets, panels, or other material) to the posts. If the rails are not attached firmly and squarely to the posts, all of your painstaking work in aligning the posts will be wasted. Remember that posts set in concrete should be left for at least 2 days before you attach rails and siding.

Joining rails to posts

Fence builders use several methods for fastening rails to posts, depending on the fence design and the materials used. Most fences use 4 by 4 posts and 2 by 4 rails, with the siding attached to the rails. With others, notably post-and-board or post-and-rail types, the rails and siding are one and the same. (Drawings of these and other fence designs appear on page 5.)

No matter what type of fence or screen you'll be building, you'll need to attach rails to posts in one of the following ways: (1) butt rails between posts; (2) lap rails over

the sides or tops of posts (be sure to make the rails long enough to span three posts for a stronger fence); (3) recess rails into post by means of a groove ("dado") or a notch; or (4) pass rails through a hole ("mortise") in the post. Dados, notches, and mortises should be cut before the posts are set. There are only two practical methods of joinery for contour hillside fencing (page 10)—lapping rails over the sides of posts, or mortising rails into them.

Joinery used for specific fence designs is further illustrated in the chapter "Projects" starting on page 61.

Because the joints between rails and posts will trap moisture, the first step—regardless of the joint you use—is to apply paint or wood preservative (see page 59) to all surfaces where the rails and posts touch, as protection against decay. This is especially important if the wood used for rails has not been pressure-treated with a preservative or is not from a decay-resistant species (see pages 15–16).

If the fence is to be painted, brush a thick coat of good-quality exterior primer on the ends of rails before attaching them to the posts. If the fence is to be stained or left unpainted, liberally coat rail ends with a colorless wood preservative such as pentachlorophenol (available at hardware and paint stores).

Butted rails. This method is typically used for fences with 4 by 4 posts and 2 by 4 rails to which wood siding is attached. Rails are cut to fit snugly between the posts, then toenailed in place with 10-penny galvanized nails. The drawing at top left of the facing page shows common methods of butting rails to posts.

For fences using 2 by 4 rails and heavy siding—such as 1-inch boards or ¾-inch plywood panels—placing the bottom rail on edge (as shown) is recommended: that way, it will prevent the fence from sagging under its own weight.

Here's the easiest way to attach the rails: Lay the rail on the ground and start the nails, driving them until their tips barely protrude through the end of the rail. Put two nails at each end of the rail, slanting them at a 45° angle about 1 inch from the end of the rail, as shown in the

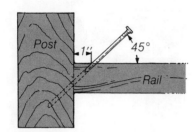

Post | 1" | 45°
Rail

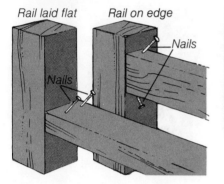

Rail laid flat | Rail on edge
Nails
Nails

drawing above. To avoid splitting the rail ends, blunt the nail tips with a hammer before nailing. If rail ends still split easily when nailed, drill nail holes with a bit two-thirds the diameter of the nail shank. With a helper holding the rail level at the other end, position the rail between the posts and drive the nails home. Use a framing square to square rails to posts as shown below.

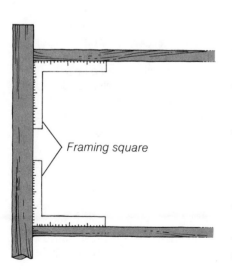

Framing square

If the bottom rail is to be laid on edge (for added strength) follow the same procedure, with this exception: at each end, drive nails through the top and bottom of the rail as shown at left.

Dadoes and notches. Recessing rails into posts by means of a notch or dado makes a stronger joint than simply butting rails between posts. In 4 by 4 posts, cut dadoes or notches no deeper than $\frac{1}{2}$ inch—otherwise the post will be weakened.

4 × 4 | 4 × 4
2 × 4 | 1/2"
2 × 4
1/2"
Dado | Notch

Notches and dadoes are more easily cut before the posts are set. To keep notches and dadoes in alignment from post to post, you must set all posts to the same height (see page 56). When you mark cutting locations on posts, always measure down from the top of the post for both top and bottom rail positions—never measure the bottom rail location from the bottom of a post.

To cut dadoes, lay posts on a flat work surface. Use a pencil and square to mark the width and depth of each dado on the post, as shown at right above. With a handsaw or power circular saw, make a series of parallel cuts across the width of the dado, then remove the wood between the outside cuts with a hammer and chisel.

To cut a notch, mark both the depth and angle on opposite sides of the post, and the width of the notch across the face of the post. With a handsaw or power circular saw, first cut the bottom edge of the notch, then make the angle cut (if using the circular saw, you'll

(see page 56)

MARKING DADO

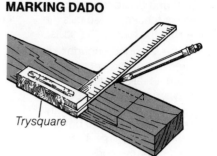

Trysquare

SAWING DADO

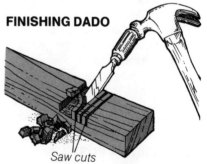

Saw cuts

FINISHING DADO

Saw cuts

need a handsaw to complete the angle cut). Cut the rail ends at an angle corresponding to that of the notch; use a pattern cut from stiff cardboard for marking angles on rail ends.

On all but the end or corner posts in the fence line, dadoes and notches are cut on both sides of the post, directly opposite each other. To attach rails to posts, slide rails into notches or dadoes and toenail into place.

Lapped rails. The easiest way to connect rails to posts is to simply lap them across the tops or sides. This method is used principally for post-and-board fences (pages 64–65) or fences whose rails run across the tops of the posts.

Use rails long enough to span three posts, and stagger joints on alternate rails, as shown in the drawing on page 64. Use nails three times as long as the thickness of the rail you'll be nailing. Where top rails meet at a corner post, miter the ends.

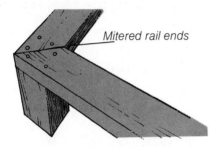
Mitered rail ends

Mortised rails. On many post-and-rail fences, rails are passed through mortises (holes) cut through the post. Posts with pre-cut mortises may be available; if not, you can make your own. Like dadoes and notches, mortises are best cut into the posts before the posts are set.

Measure all mortise locations, starting from the top of the post. To cut the mortises, lay the post across two sawhorses, mark each mortise, outline it with the drill holes, and remove remaining wood with hammer and chisel as shown

MORTISING A POST

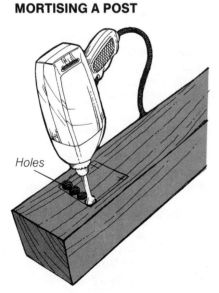
Holes

below. For more on building post-and-rail fences, see page 62.

Installing kickboards

On wood fences, the siding usually ends 6 to 8 inches above the ground to keep it from rotting at ground level. To close a gap, a kickboard is installed at the bottom of the fence before the siding is attached.

Kickboards are typically 1 by 8s or 1 by 10s of a decay-resistant wood, either centered between the posts under the bottom rail or attached to the sides of posts and bottom rail, as shown in the drawings at right. They usually extend into the ground 4 to 6 inches to help discourage animals from digging underneath the fence. Kickboards also prevent soil movement under the fence—important if you or your neighbors decide to build a raised planter bed next to the fence or otherwise change the soil level in your yards.

By attaching the kickboards to the sides of the posts (see drawing at right), you provide a ledge on which to set the siding. And if you level the kickboards when installing them, siding pieces will be kept at an even height along the fence line.

Kickboards are centered under the bottom rails when the fence design calls for sections that look

To cut: drill 1" holes through post and cut out mortise with chisel

the same on both sides. The kickboard is held in place under the bottom rail with 1 by 1 strips, as shown below.

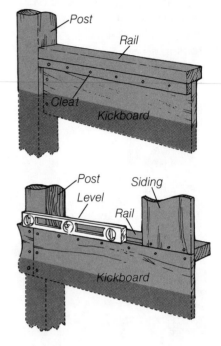

Attaching siding

How you attach siding will depend on the siding material and on your fence design.

Attaching boards, slats, pickets, or grapestakes is simple but tedious—for example, to build 100 feet of grapestake fencing, you'll be using some 1,600 nails on the siding alone. But with the driving of the last nail comes an almost indescribable feeling of satisfaction—and relief.

If you're attaching panels (plywood, hardboard, or other material) the work will go more quickly, but you'll probably need a helper to lift the panels into position and hold them steady while you do the nailing.

Attaching wire mesh to wood posts and rails requires special techniques—these are described in more detail on page 76 in the chapter "Projects."

Unless you're using decay-resistant wood, treat pickets or boards with paint or wood preservative in the same manner you treated the rails (see below). As with the rails, attaching pickets or boards while the paint is still wet will produce a more effective weather seal.

Specific techniques for attaching siding are shown in "Projects," starting on page 61.

Nailing tips. Nails used to apply wood siding to fences should be top-quality galvanized nails or aluminum nails, three times as long as the actual thickness of the siding they're expected to hold.

To avoid splitting the wood, blunt the nail tips with a hammer before using them. If you're nailing less than 1 inch from the ends of the boards or pickets, predrill the nail holes, using a bit slightly smaller than the nail shank's diameter. Remember, too, that box nails are less likely to split wood than the thicker-diameter common nails.

To keep boards, slats, or pickets in vertical alignment while attaching them to rails, use a pencil and tape measure to mark board locations on both top and bottom rails; then align boards to the marks before nailing. As you work, check vertical alignment of boards with a level.

To keep siding at an even height along the fence line, first make sure all pieces are exactly the same length. Stretch a string from post to post at the point where you want the siding to end (check it with a level), as shown in the drawing below; then align the bottoms

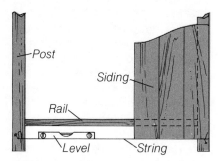

Post
Siding
Rail
Level
String

of the boards to the string. Or, if you're installing kickboards, make sure they're level, and then set the siding pieces on top of them (see facing page).

Specific techniques for attaching siding to a number of fence types

are shown in the chapter "Projects," starting on page 61.

PAINTS AND STAINS— THE FINISHING TOUCHES

Do you want to paint the fence, stain it, or let it weather naturally? First consider how you want the fence to look; then consider the ease of application and the durability of each finish.

Paint lasts longer on relatively smooth surfaces like plywood panels, surfaced boards, or metal. But stains are easier to apply on rough wood surfaces.

If you plan to retain the fence's natural wood color, you can use a clear water-sealer to extend the life of the wood. But there are no clear sealers on the market that will keep wood looking new—at least for very long. Unless painted or stained, all wood fences will eventually weather to a natural gray color.

If you find this aged look attractive, you can actually speed up the process by applying a gray stain combined with a bleaching agent— when the stain wears off, the bleaching agent, along with the action of sun and rain, will have sufficiently weathered the fence.

Paints

Paints require more work to apply than natural finishes, need more maintenance, and are more costly. However, they can do some things natural finishes cannot: create solid color effects from muted to vibrant, and permit use of lower grades of lumber in the fence since their opaque quality masks defects.

In fence painting, exterior oil-base (alkyd) and exterior latex paints have replaced the traditional whitewash of Tom Sawyer's time.

Two particular points need noting:

• Alkyd paints come in gloss, semigloss, and flat finishes. The semigloss and flat finishes are not

recommended for some wood species because they tend to absorb moisture that might lead to decay.

• Latex paints can be applied over either oil-base or water-base primers in many applications. In the section below there is a general recommendation to use oil-base primers. With redwood and western red cedar, this is absolutely imperative. Water-base primers may dissolve extractives in the wood, leading to discoloration of the paint.

For the longest lasting finish, pretreat the lumber with water repellent and apply the primer before erecting the fence. Wait two or more days between soaking the wood in water repellent and applying the primer. Primer should cover all lumber surfaces when in place, including post, rails, and siding. Apply two topcoats after the fence is completed.

Regardless of the paint type used for the topcoat, the primer should be an oil-base paint with pigments *not* containing zinc ozide. Special attention should be paid to the chemical compatibility of the water repellent, primer, and topcoat. Be sure that the manufacturer's recommendations apply specifically to the kinds of treatment and finish you are using. Using materials all from the same manufacturer is a head start on compatibility, but labels must be checked to assure workable combinations in any case.

Exterior latex paints vary greatly in price and in quality. The quality is usually determined by the amount of acrylic resin in the base—the more resin, the better.

If properly applied, a good exterior latex will hold up to the best of the oil-base paints, without cracking, oxidizing (chalking), or fading. Apply latex only to clean, relatively smooth surfaces—it won't stick to old paint that is chalking or peeling.

Old surfaces should be scraped, cleaned, and given a coat of exterior latex primer before you apply the finish coat.

Latex is easier to work with than oil-base paints because it can be washed from brushes and hands with water. Two coats will usually cover new wood. *Caution:* When painting latex over redwood, red cedar, or other "bleeding" woods, use an oil-base primer before applying the paint to prevent discoloration.

Oil-base (alkyd) paint differs from latex in that it penetrates the wood surface rather than forming a skin over it. This penetration gives oil-base paint its "sticking-power," making it preferable on semirough or previously painted surfaces. Thinning and cleanup require paint thinner or other recommended solvent.

Alkyds are the most commonly used oil-base paints today. They are durable, and do not have the unwelcome aromas of older linseed oil-base types. (Some alkyds are described on the label as alkyd-resin paints; the resin has nothing to do with the oil base, but serves as a drying agent.)

Properly applied (see below), premium latex and oil-base paints should last 8 years or longer, assuming average weather conditions. But they won't last nearly as long on rough or splintery surfaces—if you want these to look painted, use a solid color stain.

Stains

Exterior stains are applied to wood fences more often than paints, simply because they're easier to apply on rough wood surfaces and to reapply when they fade—and they're less expensive for all wood surfaces.

Within themselves, stains come in two color intensities. Semi-transparent types contain enough pigment to tint the wood surface, but not enough to hide the natural grain. Solid color stains contain more pigment, many of them appearing to be almost as opaque as paint. But stains do not cover the texture of the wood, because they penetrate rather than forming a film as paint does.

Stains come in a variety of colors ranging from pale gray through the darkest wood colors. Paint and building supply stores keep sample chips indicating colors. However, these can give only a general idea. How your choice performs will depend on your wood and your weather.

Stains must be selected carefully for technical as well as esthetic reasons. They come as both oil and water-base types. Experts recommend against water-base semi-transparent stains because they are difficult to refinish. Look for types labeled as "sealer-type" or "non-chalking." Stain should contain a mildewcide.

A recommended fence staining method is to pretreat the lumber with clear water repellent, then apply stain after the structure has been up about 60 days. (As in the case of bleaches (see below), stain will penetrate better with this or a longer wait after the water repellent has been applied.)

Heavy-bodied stains may be either brushed or sprayed on. Light-bodied types are sprayed on, then brushed smooth. (Also, light-bodied types can be applied in two coats using a brush only.)

In general, staining works best on rough or saw-textured lumber. On any surface, stains may require periodic refinishing because of wear or weathering.

Clear film finishes

Resin-base sealers, varnishes, and synthetics (polyurethanes) that form a clear film on wood surfaces are not recommended for general use on fences. Because they do not form tight bonds, such films may crack and peel from weathering over periods as short as a year. Refinishing demands tedious scraping, sanding, or application of chemical removers.

Bleaches

Bleaching is an economical and effective way to achieve rapid and uniform weathering of a fence.

Some trade-offs are involved in using bleach. It is most effective when applied to lumber *not* treated with a water repellent, which means some sacrifice in preserving or some loss of desired color effect.

In humid climates, a better choice might be a stain that produces a weathered look; see above.

If you wish to use a bleach on wood treated with a water repellent, wait 60 days after the treatment before applying the bleach; penetration will be more effective than on newly treated wood.

Apply one or two coats of bleach with a thick brush, taking care to avoid drip or lap marks. The surface must be clean and dry for application. However, once the fence is covered, periodic spraying with a hose will speed up the bleaching action. Follow the manufacturer's directions on when to wet the surface.

Applying the finish

Before applying the finish, make sure the surface is clean and dry. If you've used green (unseasoned) lumber in your fence, allow 3 weeks to a month seasoning (drying) time before painting or staining.

Paints and stains can be applied with a brush, a roller (on large, flat surfaces), or a spray gun. If you're using a roller on rough surfaces, be sure it has a 1-inch nap to assure complete coverage.

Spray guns can be rented, but they take some practice to use and are practical only for expanses of fairly solid fencing. When using a spray gun, cover nearby plants and shrubs with polyethylene sheeting to protect them from the overspray.

Because heat may create drying problems and dust, leading to marred or roughened surfaces, try to paint on a cool, windless day. In hot, dry weather, paint only after the sun is low so drying can be slow.

Before priming or painting, always sweep or dust surfaces, and be sure they are dry.

PROJECTS

Zigzag rail fence

The first fences to meander through the American frontier were made of stacked rails, rough split from the trees that pioneers cleared from their lands. Since early homestead boundary lines were loosely defined, it didn't matter that these fences took up more space than straight ones. If your space is limited, though, it may be a problem for you. You will find a photograph of a zigzag fence on page 19.

Tools and materials. Unless you want to split the rails from trees cleared off your property, look in the Yellow Pages under "Fence Materials" for the nearest source of split rails. They are generally available at lumberyards and some garden supply centers.

Common rail lengths are 6', 7', and 8'; rails vary in width, thickness, and shape. The fence shown here uses 8' rails roughly 5" by 6" square, or 5" to 6" wide if wedge-shaped (see drawing A).

Rails are stacked three high for a total fence height of 30" to 36". Each section of fence has six rails and covers a linear distance of about 11'8" if rails are laid at a 30° angle to the fence line and rail ends are overlapped 6" (see drawing B). When figuring the number of rails needed, add two 6-foot rails to the total for end posts (see drawing D).

Traditionally, the rails are simply stacked one atop the other in zigzag fashion, with the bottom rails set on flat rocks to keep them off the ground and prevent decay. But if children and animals are likely to

climb or disturb the fence, you'll need to secure the rails to each other with 6" spikes (see drawing A). Use a heavy carpenter's framing hammer to drive the spikes. To add strength to the fence, you can nail the bottom rails to wood blocks set into concrete piers set into the ground (see drawing C).

You'll need stakes and heavy string or mason's twine to plot the fence. To help you lay out rails at a

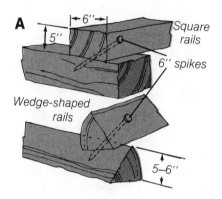

30° angle, cut a plywood template to the dimensions shown in the drawing. You'll also need two 90-pound sacks of concrete mix to set the posts at each end of the fence (see drawing D).

How to build. First plot the fence line with stake and twine, as shown in drawing B. Using the plywood template, lay down the first course of rails at 30° angles to the twine, overlapping rail ends 6". Mark the ground where rail ends cross, move the rails back slightly, and set the concrete piers (see drawing C). Attach bottom rails to the nailing blocks with 6" spikes. Stack and nail successive courses of rails. To complete the fence, attach the rails at either end to posts set in concrete, as in drawing D.

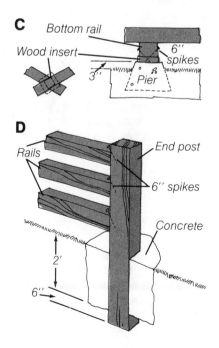

The post-and-rail fence

As trees became scarcer and property lines more exact, homesteaders straightened out the zigzag pattern of split rail fences (preceding page) by stacking rails between paired posts (see "Double post-and-rail," facing page). These double post-and-rail fences still required a considerable amount of wood, and as people gained access to tools more sophisticated than ax and sledgehammer, they built fences with fewer rails, mortising the rails into single posts (see "Mortised post-and-rail," facing page).

One variation of the mortised post-and-rail uses two or three 6" diameter poles, often with tapered rails ends mortised into square or round posts. These are commonly available as prefabricated fence kits.

For a more formal post-and-rail fence, you can use standard dimensional 4 by 4 rails set between 4 by 4 posts, as shown at the bottom of the facing page. Either dado and toenail the rails into the posts (as shown) or just toenail them between the posts. For a variation, rotate the rails 45° and toenail them between the posts.

For a source of split rails, look in the Yellow Pages under "Fence Materials." Common split rail sizes are 6', 7', and 8' long, varying in width, thickness, and shape. You'll find color photos of post-and-rail fences on pages 19 and 43.

Double post-and-rail

Though a post-and-rail fence may seem to require a lot of wood, you'll need only basic carpentry skills to build one.

Tools and materials.   The fence shown here uses split rails roughly 5" by 6" for both posts and rails. Pieces may be square, wedge-shaped, or even round, depending on what's available in your area.

The overall post length is 6'; posts are set 2½' deep, leaving 3½' above ground. Rails can be 6', 7', or 8' long, and are stacked three per fence section.

Required tools and materials include those used for plotting the fence (page 51) and for installing posts (pages 53–56). To keep the rails from being lifted from between posts, heavy-gauge metal wire is wrapped around the post tops, as shown in the drawing. Use wire cutters to cut lengths of wire, and heavy pliers to twist the wire ends.

How to build.   First plot the fence line and mark out post locations, following the directions on pages 50–53. The distance between posts should be figured so that rails overlap posts 4" to 6" at each end, as shown in the drawing.

Next, install the posts according to the directions on pages 53–56, setting them 2½' deep in the ground. To keep paired posts the proper distance apart, set one rail between them while you're back-filling each post hole with earth and gravel or concrete; then plumb each post with a level. Rails should fit snugly between posts, but not so tight that they throw the posts out of alignment.

Next, lay the first course of rails along the entire length of the fence, and then stack successive courses until the fence is complete.

Finally, wrap a length of heavy wire around the top of each pair of posts (as shown in the drawing) and tighten the wire by twisting the ends with a pair of pliers. Twisted wire ends should be left facing down and inward between posts to prevent injuries to fence climbers.

Mortised post-and-rail

There are a number of ways to mortise rails into posts, depending on the relative sizes and shapes of the posts and rails. Two of the

more common methods are described here: overlapping the rails or cutting tenons (see drawings).

Tools and materials.   The fence pictured in the drawing uses 6' long square-shaped posts, roughly 5" by 6" thick. Square split rails are roughly 3" by 4" thick and may be 6' to 8' long.

In addition to the tools and materials needed to plot the fence (page 51) and install posts (pages 53–56), you'll need an electric drill and bit, and a hammer and chisel for cutting mortises into the posts. If you use the mortise and tenon method shown in the drawing, you'll also need a handsaw for cutting tenons into the rail ends.

How to build.   Plot the fence line and mark out post locations as described on pages 50–53. The distance between posts will depend both on the length of the rails and on the method you choose (mortise-and-tenon or overlap) for mortising the rails into the posts.

Cut mortises through the wide faces of the posts *before* setting them, using the method described on page 58. Mortise positions are shown in the drawing.

The size of the mortise you should cut will depend on the width and thickness of the rails and the mortising method used.

If you're using the mortise-and-tenon method, the length of the tenon should be equal to the thickness of the post. Do not cut tenons into the ends of rails to be mortised into end or corner posts.

Install the posts, following the instructions on pages 53–56. Set the posts 2½' deep. After you set the first post, slip the ends of the rails into the mortises. Then have a helper insert the other ends of the rails into the mortises of the next post as you set it in place. Continue the same process, a section at a time, until the fence is complete.

DOUBLE POST-AND-RAIL

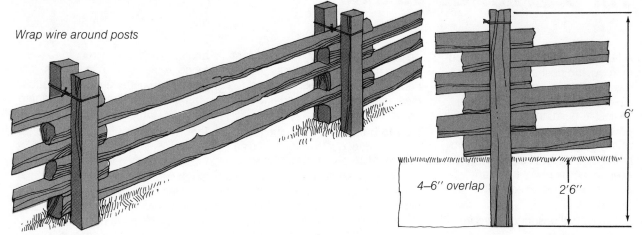

Wrap wire around posts

4–6″ overlap

6′

2′6″

MORTISED POST-AND-RAIL

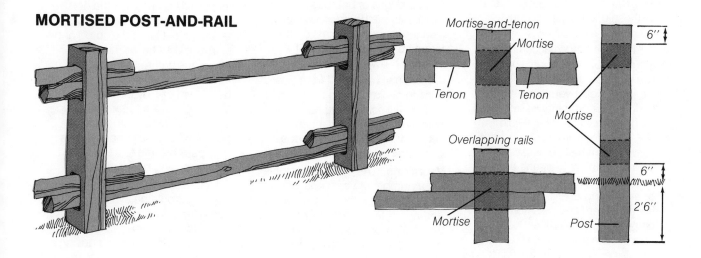

Mortise-and-tenon

Mortise

Tenon

Tenon

Mortise

Overlapping rails

Mortise

Post

6″

6″

2′6″

FORMAL POST-AND-RAIL

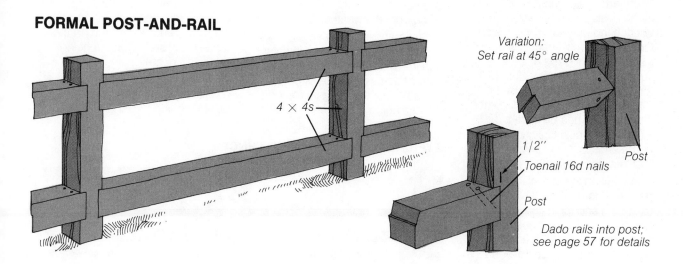

4 × 4s

Variation:
Set rail at 45° angle

Post

1/2″

Toenail 16d nails

Post

Dado rails into post;
see page 57 for details

The post-and-board fence

A familiar sight along many a country road, the post-and-board fence has traditionally been used to enclose large acreages. Among the easiest to build, these fences use perhaps the least amount of lumber of any wood fence. At today's lumber prices, the cost of rimming even an acre or two, using any other style of fence, can be prohibitive.

The typical post-and-board fence (see drawing below) is 3 to 4' high and has three rails, using 1 by 4s or 1 by 6s, attached to the sides of the posts and running parallel with the ground. Sturdier designs, such as those used to pen livestock, may use 2 by 6 rails.

But these fences accommodate a number of design variations, a few of which are shown on the facing page. Taller versions (4' to 6') are used for penning livestock and for horse corrals; lower versions (2½' to 4') are often seen in front yards of ranch-style houses or country estates. Post-and-board designs with closely spaced boards or alternating boards and slats will keep toddlers and pets from slipping through the fence. Post-and-board fences adapt especially well to hillsides and rolling terrain (for a discussion of hillside fencing, see page 10).

Tools and materials. The sizes of the posts and boards you use will depend on your fence design. Ordinarily, if post spacing is 6' or less, you'll use posts 4" by 4" square or 4" in diameter if round; for post spacing over 6', use posts 6" by 6" square or 6" in diameter if round. Use boards twice the length of the post spacing so that board ends fall on alternate posts (see drawing at right).

In addition to the tools and materials used for plotting the fence (page 51) and for installing posts (pages 53–56), you'll need a steel tape measure, a pencil and try square for marking board locations

on posts, and a heavy hammer for driving nails. For 1" boards, use 8-penny galvanized nails to fasten them to posts; for 2" boards, use 16-penny nails.

How to build. First plot the fence line and mark out post locations as described on pages 50–53; then install the posts, following instructions on pages 53–56. For long stretches of fence, you may find it more convenient to use the successive method of setting posts described on page 55.

Using a tape measure, pencil, and try square, mark posts where the top edges of boards will cross them. Nail the boards to the posts, staggering the end joints on alternate posts, as shown in the drawing below.

Drive nails about 1" from board ends to avoid splitting the wood. If boards still split during nailing, blunt the nail tips with a hammer before driving them; if that doesn't work, predrill nail holes.

Variations. As mentioned, there are a number of variations (see facing page) on the simple post-and-board fence shown below. Some of these serve purposes other than simply adding visual interest to the fence. The post top and side details, shown on the facing page, for example, not only are decorative, but help protect the fence from the weather.

Cutting post tops at an angle as shown helps them shed rainwater and forestalls decay. Attaching a cap rail across the tops of posts helps protect the entire fence from the damaging effects of rain, snow,

and sun, and adds strength to the fence. A slanted cap rail sheds water even better and discourages young fence walkers. If you want to conserve lumber, consider simple post caps—they offer some weather protection to posts and rail joints.

Battens nailed to the sides of posts over boards help protect board ends from the weather and serve to prevent boards from working loose from the posts. Battens and cap rails in tandem add a finishing touch.

Corral fencing. Post-and-board fences still seem to be the horse-owner's favorite for corrals. Corral fencing must be tall (5' to 6') and sturdy. If your horse has a rambunctious nature, you may find it advisable to use sturdier rails—2 by 6s instead of 1 by 6s. Boards should be nailed to the corral sides of posts to avoid the danger of horses hitting their shoulders as they pass by, and to keep them from knocking boards loose.

Diagonal board patterns or cross bracing should be avoided on corral fences and gates, as a pawing horse can get a hoof caught where boards intersect, causing injury. It's also a good idea to block off the fence corners, particularly if there's more than one horse in the corral or pasture. This will prevent a horse from being cornered and injured by another, or hurt on the fence itself (see "Corral fencing" on facing page).

Refer to the chapter on gates (pages 88–95) for information on designing and building gates.

TYPICAL POST-AND-BOARD FENCE

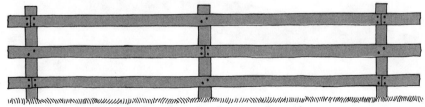

Boards span 3 posts; stagger rails as shown

FOUR POST-AND-BOARD STYLES

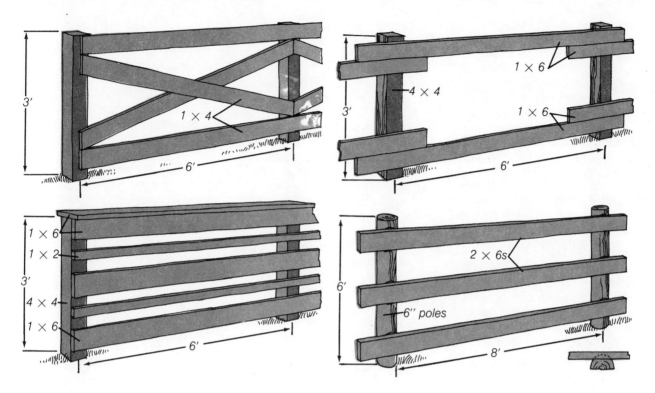

3'
1 × 4
6'

1 × 6
4 × 4
3'
1 × 6
6'

1 × 6
1 × 2
3'
4 × 4
1 × 6
6'

2 × 6s
6'
6" poles
8'

POST TOP AND SIDE DETAILS

Slanted post top

30°

4 × 4

Post cap
2 × 6 × 6

Slanted cap

1 × 6
Cap rail

1" siding

30°

4 × 4 Post

1 × 6
Cap rail

1" siding

4 × 4 Post

1 × 6

1 × 4
batten

4 × 4

Cap rail and batten

CORRAL FENCING

6 × 6   1 × 6

5'

8'

The picket fence

Traditionally, the picket fence has been associated with colonial architecture, but today it's found with almost any type of house, whether in the city or in the country. The wide range of picket and post top treatments allows the builder to give each fence an individual character while keeping within the boundaries of traditional design. A few of these treatments are shown below. You'll find more examples on pages 22–23 in the color section of this book.

Tools and materials. The typical picket fence (see facing page) is about 3′ high, with 4 by 4 posts on 6′ centers and 2 by 4 rails nailed flat between them. Overall post length is 5′ (3′ above ground and 2′ below). Pickets are usually 1 by 3s spaced 2½″ apart, though other sizes and spacings may be used.

Most lumber dealers and fence suppliers do not carry ready-made pickets—those that do will offer only a limited choice in picket designs. Many dealers will cut boards to picket length, usually for a small cutting fee.

You'll most likely have to cut the picket top designs yourself or have a cabinet shop or woodworker do the work. The latter choice may be preferable if you have very many pickets to cut, or if the design you want is an intricate one. Cutting post tops is also best left to an experienced woodworker for all but the simplest of designs.

Take the woodworker a sample picket with the top design traced on it in pencil. If possible, get esti-mates from several shops for the work to be done.

If you cut the pickets yourself, use a handsaw or power circular saw for cutting simple pointed pickets, a saber saw for cutting more intricate designs. You'll also need C-clamps c wood clamps if you'll be cutting more than one picket at a time (see "Cutting pickets," facing pa).

You may wish to add a kick-board along the bottom of the fence. Kickboards for picket fences are usually nailed to the sides of the posts so that pickets rest on top of the boards (see "Kickboard detail" on facing page). For informa-tion on installing kickboards, see page 58.

In addition to the tools and mate-rials needed for plotting the fence line (page 51), installing the posts (pages 53–57), and cutting the pickets, you'll need a try square and pencil for marking rail loca-tions on posts and squaring pickets on the rails, and a hammer and nails for attaching rails and pickets. Use 10-penny galvanized nails for toenailing 2 by 4 rails to 4 by 4 posts; 7-penny nails for nailing 1″ pickets to rails.

How to build. First plot the fence line and lay out post locations as described on pages 50–53. Before starting the actual construction, cut all of the picket tops and, if your design calls for it, the post tops as well.

If you're cutting your own pickets, lay them flat across two sawhorses or on a workbench to do the cutting. For simple pointed pickets, you can use either a hand-saw or power circular saw; for more intricate designs, use a saber saw (see "Cutting pickets," facing page). After you've cut the first picket, use it as a pattern for mark-ing the rest.

To save time, you can cut two pickets at once (three, if you're using a portable circular saw) by sandwiching them together with clamps, as shown in the drawing. To make perfectly matched pickets, pieces must be perfectly aligned while being cut, and saw cuts must be exactly vertical.

Once all of the pickets are cut, install the posts as described on pages 53–56; then toenail the rails in place, following the instructions on pages 56–58. If your fence will have a kickboard, install it next (see page 58 for details).

The final step is to attach the pickets. Nail the first picket in place, checking it with a try square against the rail for square.

To ensure uniform height and spacing of successive pickets, make a spacer slat as shown on the facing page. Cut the slat to the exact length of the pickets and attach a small cleat to the back so that when it's hung on the top rail, the slat will be at an even height with the pickets, as shown.

Position the slat alongside the first picket, then place the next picket against it. Align the bottoms of picket and slat, and nail the picket in place. Remove the slat and repeat the process.

PICKETS   **POSTS**

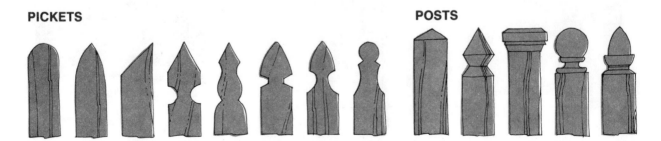

TYPICAL PICKET FENCE

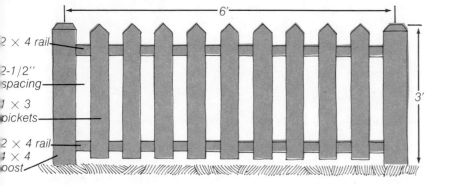

2 × 4 rail

2-1/2''
spacing

1 × 3
pickets

2 × 4 rail
4 × 4
post

6'

3'

KICKBOARD DETAIL

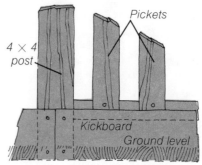

Pickets

4 × 4
post

Kickboard
Ground level

FOUR PICKET FENCES

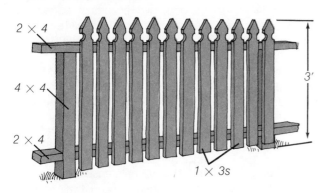

2 × 4

4 × 4

2 × 4

1 × 3s

3'

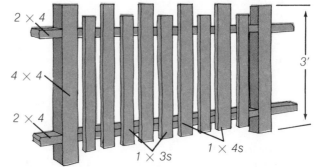

2 × 4

4 × 4

2 × 4

1 × 3s

1 × 4s

3'

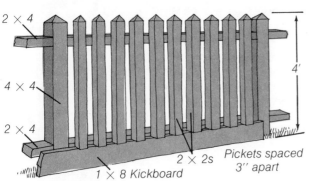

2 × 4

4 × 4

2 × 4

2 × 2s

1 × 8 Kickboard

Pickets spaced
3'' apart

4'

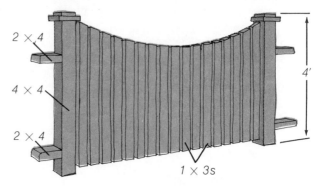

2 × 4

4 × 4

2 × 4

1 × 3s

4'

SPACING PICKETS

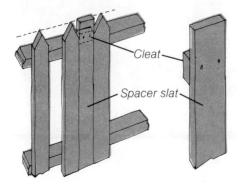

Cleat

Spacer slat

CUTTING PICKETS

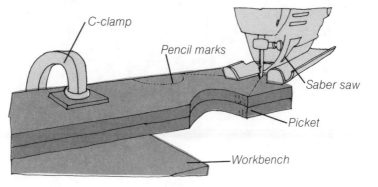

C-clamp

Pencil marks

Saber saw

Picket

Workbench

The board fence

There's an almost unlimited range of designs and variations of board fences. Just a few of the many styles are shown on the facing page.

Board fences serve a number of purposes and are easily built, but they must be thoughtfully designed and placed to overcome a number of disadvantages. Solid board fences are expensive because they require a great deal of lumber. They offer maximum privacy, but too often create a boxed-in feeling. Before you choose a style, read the planning chapter of this book thoroughly (see pages 4–17) and decide what you want your fence to do.

On variations with the boards nailed to one side of the frame, the fence will have a "good" side and a "bad" side. As a courtesy you may want to face the "good" side toward your neighbor's property, with the frame side facing yours. If you can talk your neighbor into sharing the cost of the fence, you might agree on a design that alternates the panels. There are a number of ways to dress up the frame side of the fence—some are shown on page 83. The best solution, of course, is to design a board fence that looks good on both sides.

These are often referred to as "good neighbor fences." In addition to the fences shown at right, you'll find color photos of board fences on pages 24–26 and 34.

Tools and materials. The typical board fence (shown below) is 6′ high, with a frame of 4 by 4 posts set on 6′ centers and 2 by 4 rails nailed between the posts. The posts are 8′ long and are set in concrete, 2′ deep in the ground. To help support the weight of the boards, the bottom rail is sometimes placed on edge unless a kickboard is installed.

Kickboards are installed along the bottom of a fence to close the gap between the fence and the ground. They are made from 1″-thick lumber and may be nailed to the undersides of the bottom rails, or nailed to the faces of the posts and bottom rails. Face-nailing the kickboard is the easiest method and provides the siding boards with support. The kickboard should span at least three posts for strength.

Tools needed to build this fence include those used for plotting the fence line and locating posts (page 51), installing posts (pages 53–56), and attaching rails, kickboards, and siding (pages 56–58). Use

nails three times as long as the thickness of the boards you'll be fastening.

How to build. First plot the fence line and lay out post locations as described on pages 50–53; then install the posts, following the instructions on pages 53–56. Next, join the rails to the posts and attach the kickboards, following the instructions on pages 56–58. For the basic fence shown below, you can attach the boards by following the general directions on page 58. Leave a slight gap between boards to allow for expansion during the wet season.

To attach horizontal siding, start with the bottom board. Position the board and fasten one end with a single nail. Place a level on top of the board and adjust the board until it is absolutely level. Finish nailing the board to the posts and rail. This will help ensure that successive boards above it will also be level.

To add a little character to the basic board fence shown at left below, you can cut the ends of the top board to one of the patterns shown in the drawing at right below. It is, of course, easier to cut the board tops before attaching them to the fence.

TYPICAL BOARD FENCE

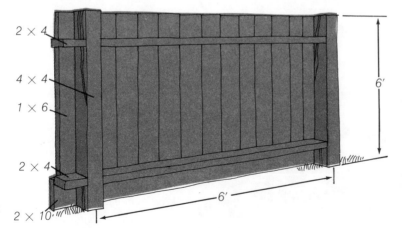

2 × 4

4 × 4

1 × 6

2 × 4

2 × 10

6′

6′

TOP DESIGNS

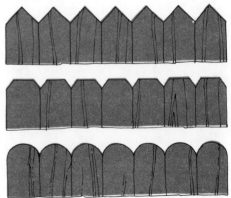

TWELVE BOARD FENCES

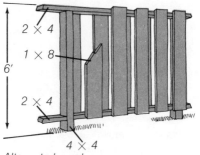

Alternate boards

2 × 4
1 × 8
2 × 4
6'
4 × 4

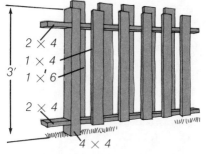

Alternate widths (opposite sides)

2 × 4
1 × 4
1 × 6
2 × 4
3'
4 × 4

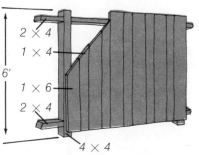

Alternate widths (same side)

2 × 4
1 × 4
1 × 6
2 × 4
6'
4 × 4

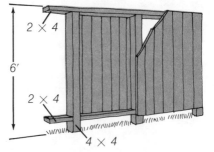

Alternate panels

2 × 4
2 × 4
6'
4 × 4

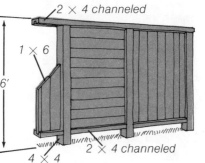

Vertical & horizontal

2 × 4 channeled
1 × 6
2 × 4 channeled
6'
4 × 4

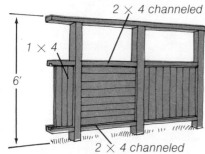

Vertical & horizontal (open top)

2 × 4 channeled
1 × 4
6'
2 × 4 channeled

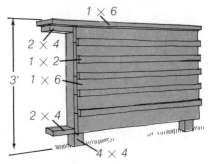

Horizontal board & batten

1 × 6
2 × 4
1 × 2
1 × 6
2 × 4
3'
4 × 4

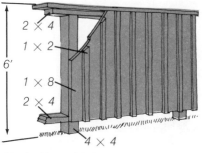

Vertical board & batten

2 × 4
1 × 2
1 × 8
2 × 4
6'
4 × 4

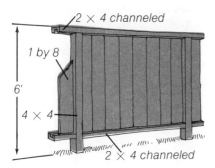

Good neighbor (same both sides)

2 × 4 channeled
1 by 8
4 × 4
6'
2 × 4 channeled

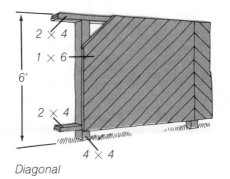

Diagonal

2 × 4
1 × 6
2 × 4
6'
4 × 4

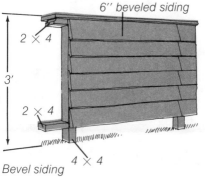

Bevel siding

2 × 4
2 × 4
6'' beveled siding
3'
4 × 4

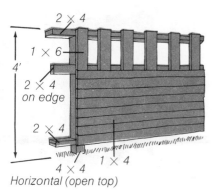

Horizontal (open top)

2 × 4
1 × 6
2 × 4 on edge
2 × 4
4 × 4   1 × 4
4'

The louver fence

Louver fences have the advantage of providing privacy without substantially restricting the flow of air through a yard or garden. Depending on the direction (vertical or horizontal), spacing, and angle of the louvers, they can control the amount of sunlight falling on plants near the fence, and temper harsh winds, yet limit or completely block the view from outside into a yard.

Horizontal louvers placed with their "blind side" toward the public allow those inside the fence to see out, but block the view from the outside. Vertical louvers offer "progressive privacy"—that is, only a small portion of the yard is fully visible to anyone walking past.

Louver fences are relatively expensive because they require more material per running foot than a solid board fence of the same height. Also, louvers should be of kiln-dried lumber to minimize warping and sagging. In addition, above average carpentry skills are needed to assure that the fence parts fit properly. Needless to say, these fences should be used in fairly short runs and placed judiciously to take full advantage of their functions.

Tools and materials. The two louver fences shown below are 6' tall, with louvers set at a 45 degree angle. Posts are 8'-long 4 by 4s, set in concrete on 4' centers, 2' feet deep. Top rails are 8'-long 2 by 4s, spanning three post tops; bottom rails, 3' 8½'' long, are toenailed between posts. Louvers for the horizontal louver fence are kiln-dried 1 by 6s, the same length as the bottom rails; for the vertical louver fence, 1 by 6 louvers are slightly under 5' long.

To determine the actual height of the louvers for your vertical louver fence, measure the distance between the top and bottom rails after you have built the fence. For accuracy, make the measurements along the inside faces of the posts. You will find the louvers easier to install if you cut them ⅛'' shorter than this dimension.

Kickboards of 2 by 10 lumber are fastened to the bottom rails and posts of the vertical louver fence to help support the louvers.

Spacers for both fences are cut from 1 by 3s; you'll need a combination square and pencil to mark 45° angles on the spacers.

Tools needed for both fences include those used for plotting the fence line and locating posts (page 51), installing posts (pages 53–57), and adding rails and siding (pages 57–59). Use nails three times as long as the thickness of the boards you'll be fastening.

How to build. First plot the fence line and mark out post locations as described on page 51; then install the posts, following the instructions on pages 53–57. Next, join the rails to the posts, following instructions on page 57.

If you're building the vertical louver fence shown below, install the kickboard before attaching the siding. Nail the kickboards to the posts and bottom rails.

For vertical louvers: First cut 1'' by 4'' spacers to the dimensions shown below. Cut one of the spacers in half (see top view in drawing) and nail the half spacers to the top and bottom rails against a post. Position the first louver against the spacers and toenail into the rails. Butt spacers against the louver, top and bottom, and nail to rails. Add another louver and repeat the process.

For horizontal siding: First cut 1'' by 3'' spacers to the dimensions shown below. Cut one of the spacers in half (see end view in drawing) and nail the half spacers to two successive posts against the bottom rail. Position the first louver against the spacers and toenail into the posts. Butt spacers against the louver at both ends and nail to posts. Add another louver and repeat the process.

VERTICAL LOUVER FENCE　　　　　　**HORIZONTAL LOUVER FENCE**

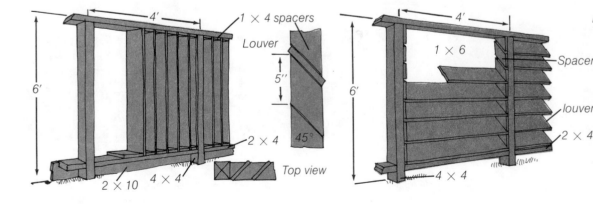

The basketweave fence

This fence is popular with do-it-yourselfers because it is easy to construct, requires a minimum of materials for a solid barrier, and has a pleasing interwoven design with attractive patterns of shadows. Two basic designs are shown below—the horizontal basketweave and the vertical basketweave.

Because the strips are relatively thin to permit weaving, this fence often works better in mild climates; harsh weather conditions can rapidly deteriorate the wood. The horizontal version should be avoided if there are young fence climbers about—it makes a perfect stepladder, and the wood strips are easily damaged by young hands and feet.

Tools and materials. The two fences shown below are 6′ tall. Posts are 8′-long 4 by 4s, on 4′ centers, set 2′ deep in concrete. Top rails are 8′-long 2 by 4s, each one spanning three post tops; bottom rails, 3′ 8½″ long, are toenailed between posts.

Both fences use ½ by 6 wood strips for siding; these are nailed to 1 by 2 nailing strips, and attached to either post or rails, depending on the version being built (see drawings below).

The horizontal version has 1 by 1 spacers positioned midway between the posts around which the wood strips are woven. The vertical version has 2 by 2s toenailed to posts midway between the top and bottom rails, as shown.

To build either of these fences, you'll need tools for plotting the fence line and locating posts (page 51), installing posts (pages 53–56), and attaching rails and siding (pages 56–58). Use nails three times as long as the thickness of the rails and boards you'll be fastening.

How to build. First plot the fence line and mark out post locations as described on pages 50–53; then install the posts, following instructions on pages 53–56. Next, join the rails to the posts according to the instructions on pages 56–58.

For vertical basketweave: First center and nail 1 by 2 nailing strips to top and bottom rails, as shown in the drawing (bottom left). Next, toenail 2 by 2s between the posts, midway between the top and bottom rails.

The ½ by 6 strips must be cut long enough to allow weaving around the 2 by 2s. Cut a strip about 2″ longer than the distance between the rails; then cut off one end, ¼″ at a time, until the strip fits properly. Use it as a pattern for cutting the rest of the strips. Weave ½ by 6 strips around the 2 by 2s, nailing them to the 1 by 2s as shown. Finally, attach the strips to the 2 by 2s with 4-penny nails.

For horizontal basketweave: First center and nail 1 by 2 nailing strips to posts as shown (below right). Next, nail ½ by 6 strips to the 1 by 2s, alternating sides as shown in the drawing. Finally, thread the 1 by 1 through the strips, centering it between the posts to create a basketweave. You may find it easier to do this before nailing the top rail to the posts.

VERTICAL BASKETWEAVE FENCE

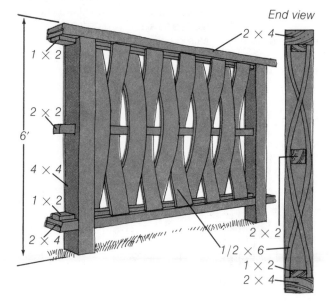

HORIZONTAL BASKETWEAVE FENCE

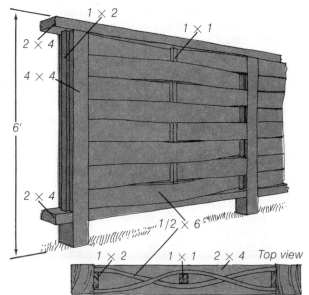

The grapestake fence

Rough-split redwood stakes, used for propping up grapevines in vineyards, have long been a popular material for making fences with a rustic look.

Grapestake fences are more common in the western United States than in other parts of the country because redwood stakes are more accessible in the West. Their counterpart east of the Rockies is the stockade fence (see photo on page 20), which uses round, pointed stakes or poles 2″ to 3″ in diameter. Building methods for both fences are the same.

The most common type of grapestake fencing consists of stakes nailed vertically to the side of a standard fence frame of 4 by 4 posts and 2 by 4 rails, as shown below. Left unpainted, the stakes will weather to a soft, silvery gray that provides a natural-looking backdrop for plantings and complements the warm tones of brick and stonework in the garden.

The versatile grapestake can be used to create a number of fence designs, high or low, formal or informal. A few of these are shown on the facing page. The narrow stakes are especially suitable for hillside fencing (page 10) and curved fencing (page 11). Photos of several grapestake fences appear on page 21 in the color section of this book.

Some disadvantages: grapestakes have a splintery surface that some people object to; others might not want the natural, weathered look of such fences and will find the rough stakes difficult to paint. Solid grapestake fencing is also expensive, and though the stakes are easy to handle, building the fence can become tedious—in erecting 100′ of solid grapestake fencing, you'll drive more nails than you would to attach siding to a five-room house.

Tools and materials. Grapestakes are about 2″ square, and 3′ to 6′ in length. Because they're split from redwood logs, they have irregular, splintery edges (you may want to wear heavy gloves when handling them). They were originally split from heartwood, but there is a trend today toward the use of sapwood, which has a tendency to decay rapidly when placed in the ground.

Grapestakes are available either in the full 2″ by 2″ size, or more commonly as 1 by 2 slats (cut lengthwise from 2″ by 2″ stock) with one rough side and one fairly smooth side for easier nailing. The latter size is more economical and easier to work with when nailing against 2 by 4 rails.

The fence shown below uses 8′-long 4 by 4 posts set on 6′ centers, 2′ in the ground and in concrete. Rails are 2 by 4s toenailed between posts. Unless you're installing a kickboard (page 58), you'll need a 6′ length of straight 1 by 4 nailed temporarily to the posts to align the stake bottoms as shown below.

Tools needed include those for plotting the fence line (page 51), installing posts (pages 53–56), and attaching rails and siding (pages 56–58). Use nails three times as long as the thickness of the grapestakes you'll be nailing.

How to build. The fence shown below, like most grapestake variations, uses a standard fence frame of 4 by 4 posts and 2 by 4 rails. The first step is to plot the fence line and lay out post locations as described on pages 50–53. Next, install the posts, following the instructions on pages 53–56.

Once all of the posts are set, attach the rails to them according to the instructions on pages 56–58. Because of the weight of the grapestakes, you may want to set the bottom rail on edge to keep it from sagging.

When the frame is complete, begin attaching the stakes, starting at one end of the fence. Depending on how you want the fence top to look, you can attach stakes with the pointed end up or down. Unless you're using a kickboard, temporarily nail a 6′-long 1 by 4 between the posts at the bottom of the fence and rest the stakes on it as you nail them. Use a 2′ carpenter's level to level the 1 by 4, as shown, so that stake tops will line up level.

Nail the first stake to the frame, checking it with the level to make sure it's vertical. Because grapestakes are irregular in shape, check with a level every fourth or fifth stake as you're nailing to make sure you're attaching them on the vertical. If you find the stakes have started to slant, you can compensate by adjusting the tops or bottoms of a few stakes until they're all running vertically again.

TYPICAL GRAPESTAKE FENCE

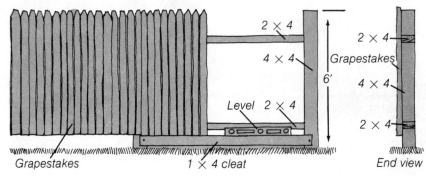

Grapestakes 2 × 4 4 × 4 6' Level 2 × 4 Grapestakes 1 × 4 cleat 2 × 4 2 × 4 4 × 4 2 × 4 End view

TEN GRAPESTAKE VARIATIONS

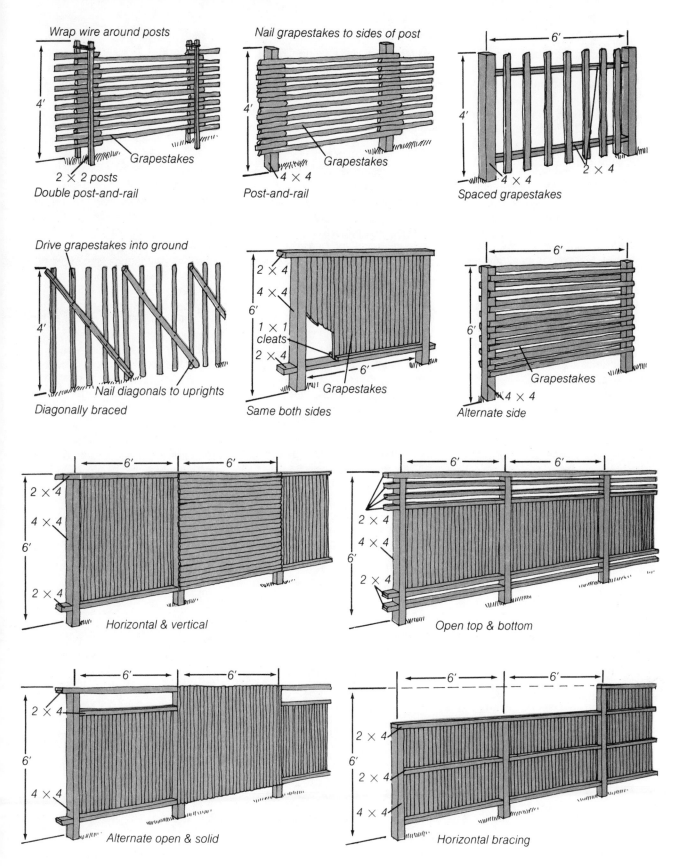

Wrap wire around posts

4'

Grapestakes

2 × 2 posts

Double post-and-rail

Nail grapestakes to sides of post

4'

Grapestakes

4 × 4

Post-and-rail

6'

4'

4 × 4   2 × 4

Spaced grapestakes

Drive grapestakes into ground

4'

Nail diagonals to uprights

Diagonally braced

2 × 4

4 × 4

6'

1 × 1
cleats

2 × 4

6'

Grapestakes

Same both sides

6'

6'

Grapestakes

4 × 4

Alternate side

6'   6'

2 × 4

4 × 4

6'

2 × 4

Horizontal & vertical

6'   6'

2 × 4

4 × 4

6'

2 × 4

Open top & bottom

6'   6'

2 × 4

6'

4 × 4

Alternate open & solid

6'   6'

2 × 4

2 × 4

6'

4 × 4

Horizontal bracing

The panel fence

Fences and screens built with panels have several advantages. If solid, they can offer maximum privacy (though it may seem confining at times); when translucent, panel fences have a light, airy appearance; they can even be transparent, for the sake of a view. All panel fences provide a measure of wind protection (see page 7). They can be built to afford full shade, full sun or anything in between, depending on their orientation and on choice of material. And once the fence frame is complete, panels can be quickly installed.

Panels are available in plywood with a variety of finishes—smooth, rough sawn, simulated siding, stucco, shingled, and even stone; other panels are of hardboard, clear and translucent plastic, and clear and translucent glass (see pages 13–15).

Panel fences require strong structural support, not only because of the weight of materials in the case of plywood and glass, but also because a solid panel fence must withstand the force of the wind. Make sure that at least one-third of the post length is in the ground and set in concrete.

If you're considering a glass fence or screen, get professional assistance. The supporting structure must be rigid so that the glass cannot be twisted, causing breakage; it must also be designed to accommodate the expansion and contraction of the glass. Glass panel fences are often built on a low masonry wall to provide the necessary sturdiness (see below).

Tools and materials. Plywood, hardboard, plastic, and glass are available in a variety of thicknesses and sizes (see page 13 for information on plywood and hardboard panel thicknesses; page 15 for information on plastic and glass). The thickness of the plastic or glass you should use will depend on the size of each fence panel. Consult the manufacturer or supplier or a professional for advice on the best thickness for your fence.

Tools needed to build a panel fence include those used for plotting the fence line and laying out posts (page 51), installing posts (pages 53–56), and attaching rails, kickboards, and siding (pages 56–58). Use nails three times as long as the thickness of the material you're fastening.

If building a fence with glass or plastic, you'll find it more convenient to have the panels cut to size by the supplier.

How to build. First plot the fence line and indicate post locations as described on pages 50–53; then install the posts according to the instructions on pages 53–56. Except for the freestanding screen at right, you'll need top and bottom rails; so next join the rails—and the kickboard if you're adding one—to the posts as described on pages 56–58. The plywood panel for the freestanding screen at right is attached directly to the posts and a frame is built around it.

For the other fences shown on the right, the plywood panels can be nailed to the face of the frame or inserted in the frame and held in place with strips. Plastic panels can also be installed either way; if you're nailing plastic, predrill nail holes in the panels to avoid cracking. Large glass panels are awkward and dangerous to handle, and cutting and installation should be left to professionals.

A few words on finishing plywood panels. Even though you're using exterior grade plywood, the faces and especially the edges should be sealed with paint or another good exterior finish. If you can design your fence so that plywood edges are protected from the weather, so much the better.

GLASS SCREEN

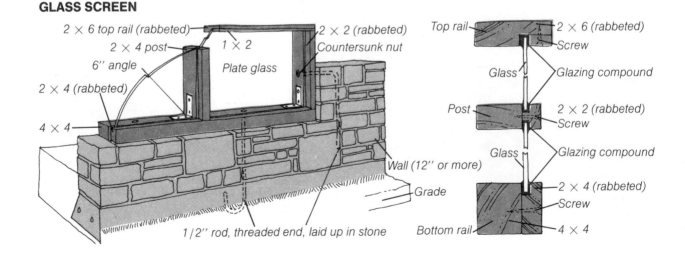

2 × 6 top rail (rabbeted)
2 × 4 post
6″ angle
2 × 4 (rabbeted)
4 × 4
1 × 2
Plate glass
2 × 2 (rabbeted)
Countersunk nut
Wall (12″ or more)
Grade
1/2″ rod, threaded end, laid up in stone

Top rail
Glass
Post
Glass
Bottom rail
2 × 6 (rabbeted)
Screw
Glazing compound
2 × 2 (rabbeted)
Screw
Glazing compound
2 × 4 (rabbeted)
Screw
4 × 4

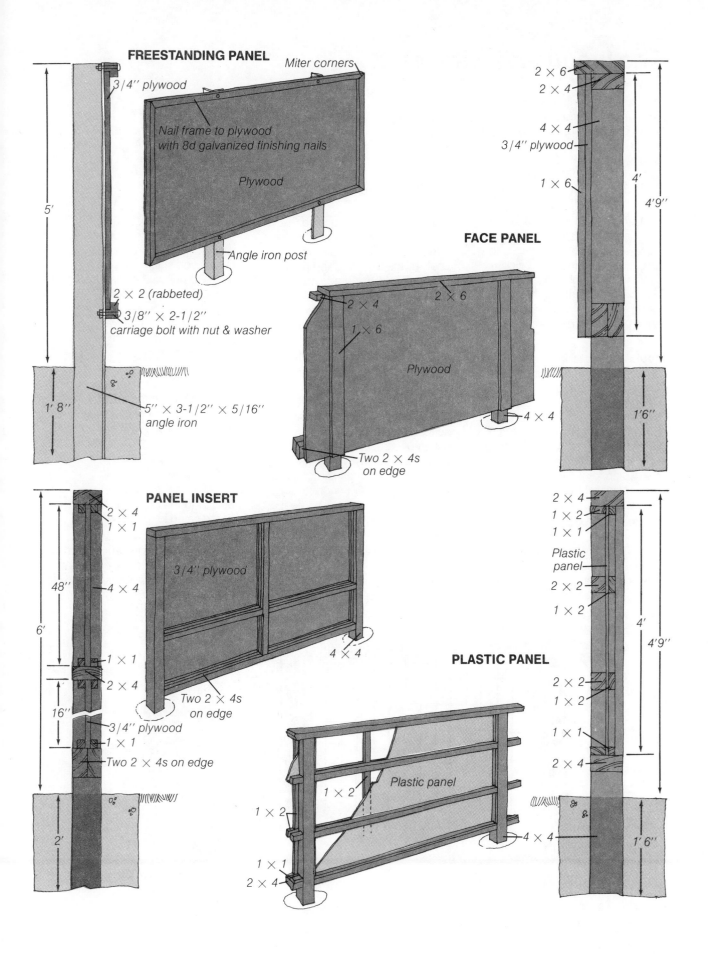

FREESTANDING PANEL

3/4'' plywood

Miter corners

Nail frame to plywood with 8d galvanized finishing nails

Plywood

5'

Angle iron post

2 × 2 (rabbeted)

3/8'' × 2-1/2'' carriage bolt with nut & washer

1' 8''

5'' × 3-1/2'' × 5/16'' angle iron

FACE PANEL

2 × 4

2 × 6

1 × 6

Plywood

4 × 4

Two 2 × 4s on edge

2 × 6
2 × 4

4 × 4

3/4'' plywood

1 × 6

4'

4'9''

1'6''

PANEL INSERT

2 × 4
1 × 1

3/4'' plywood

48''

4 × 4

6'

1 × 1

2 × 4

Two 2 × 4s on edge

4 × 4

16''

3/4'' plywood
1 × 1

Two 2 × 4s on edge

2'

PLASTIC PANEL

Plastic panel

1 × 2

1 × 2

1 × 1

2 × 4

2 × 4
1 × 2
1 × 1

Plastic panel

2 × 2

1 × 2

2 × 2
1 × 2

1 × 1

2 × 4

4'

4'9''

4 × 4

1'6''

The wood and wire fence

Wire mesh of various kinds has many practical applications in fencing. Heavy wire mesh provides security and offers a support for climbing plants without blocking out a view. Chain link fencing is popular for residential security.

Most wire and chain link fences use metal posts and require professional installation. The fence shown here, though, can easily be constructed by the home handyperson with the aid of a strong helper. A wood and wire fence is pictured on page 42 in the color section of this book.

Tools and materials. The fence shown below consists of 2″ by 4″ welded wire mesh attached to a wood frame of 4 by 4 posts and 2 by 4 rails. The wire mesh is sold in 50′ and 100′ rolls in 3′, 4′, and 6′ widths. Though the fence shown uses the 4′ width, you can adapt the design to a 3′ or 6′ fence. You might also want to substitute a tighter 2″ by 2″ mesh.

The 4 by 4 posts, 6′ long, are set on 6′ centers, 18″ deep and in concrete. Top rails of 12′-long 2 by 4s span three post tops. Bottom rails, 5′8½″ long, are toenailed between posts. A 1 by 6 cap is nailed to the top rail to give the fence a more finished appearance; and 1 by 8 kickboards are nailed across the posts to the bottom rails to help hold the wire in place and to keep small animals from crawling under the fence.

Tools needed for building this fence include those used for plotting the fence line and laying out posts (page 51), installing posts (pages 53–56), and adding rails (pages 56–58). Use nails three times as long as the thickness of the wood members you'll be fastening. The wire is fastened to the posts and rails with ¾″ staples driven with a hammer (see drawing below).

How to build. First plot the fence line and post locations as described on pages 50–53. Posts are set on 6′ centers as indicated in the drawing below. Next, install posts, following the instructions on pages 53–56; use concrete fill. When the concrete has hardened, join the rails to the posts, following the instructions on pages 56–58. To complete the frame, center the 1 by 6 cap over the top rail and nail it in place.

To attach the wire to the frame, start at one end of the fence and unroll enough to cover two sections (about 12′). Align the top of the wire mesh with the underside of the 1 by 6 cap as shown in the drawing.

Next, attach the wire to the first post, driving staples at the top, center, and bottom. Then have your helper stretch the wire mesh taut as you staple the wire to the next two posts, checking frequently to make sure the wire stays in alignment. Once the wire is tacked in place over the first two sections, go back and secure the wire to posts and rails by driving staples every 6″.

Repeat the whole process until you reach the end of the fence. If you should run out of wire before reaching the end of the fence, splice a new roll by overlapping the meshes on a post as shown in the drawing.

Finally, nail the 1 by 8 kickboards to the bottom of the fence as indicated in the drawing.

If you wish to give the fence a more finished appearance, you can nail 1 by 4 strips to the posts and 1 by 2 strips to the top rail to cover the staples.

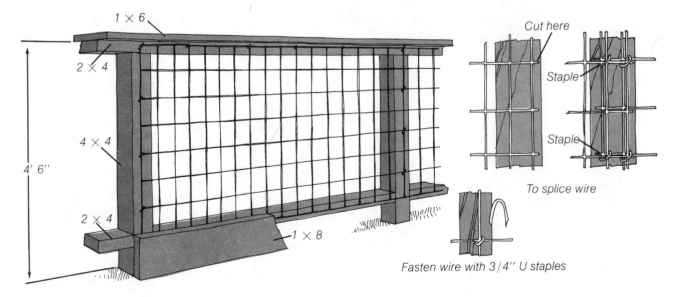

1 × 6

2 × 4

4 × 4

4′ 6″

2 × 4

1 × 8

Cut here

Staple

Staple

To splice wire

Fasten wire with 3/4″ U staples

Lattice screen

Lattice screens and fences are light, airy structures, commonly associated with Victorian architecture. They can be used for several purposes in the yard. A tightly woven lattice can be used to screen out an objectionable view while allowing air to flow into the yard. Widely spaced latticework will preserve a view, serve as a traffic director, or provide a backdrop for tall plantings. See page 79 for more garden screen projects.

Because of their light weight and open design, lattice screens can be built as tall as 8' without need of heavy framing or bracing.

Latticework usually consists of thin lath, crisscrossed horizontally and vertically or on the diagonal. The screen shown here is only one of many popular designs. You'll find pictures of lattice fences and screens on pages 28–29 in the color section of this book.

Tools and materials. The screen shown here uses ¼" by 1½" lath. You'll need nine pieces 8' long and seventeen pieces 5'5½" long for

every 8' of screen. Posts are 8'-long 2 by 4s set 2' in the ground, in concrete, on 4' centers.

Top rails are 8'-long 2 by 4s nailed across three post tops; bottom rails, 3'10½" long, are butted between posts.

Tools needed include those used for plotting the fence (page 51), installing posts (pages 53–56), and adding rails and lath siding (pages 56–58). Use nails three times as long as the thickness of the boards and lath you'll be fastening. A backsaw and miter box come in handy for making square, clean cuts in lath strips.

How to build. First plot the fence line and lay out post locations as described on pages 50–53; posts are set on 4' centers as shown in the drawing below. Next, install the posts according to the instructions on pages 53–56. Set posts in concrete.

When the concrete has hardened, join the rails to the posts, following the instructions on pages 56–58. If you wish to paint the

screen, it's easier to paint the frame and individual lath strips before joining them.

Attach the first vertical lath strip to the face of the first post, as shown in the drawing. Space successive vertical strips 6½" apart, measuring and marking their locations on top and bottom rails. Use one nail at top and one at bottom to attach each strip.

Once all of the vertical strips are nailed to the frame, attach the first horizontal strip along the face of the bottom rail, over the vertical strips. Space successive horizontal strips 6½" apart, measuring and marking their locations on the posts. Use one nail at each end to attach strips to posts. The last strip should end up directly over the face of the top rail.

Once you've finished one 8' section, go on to the next. When all of the horizontal strips are fastened, you may wish to protect the lath ends by nailing vertical strips over the joints. This will also help keep the lath ends from working loose.

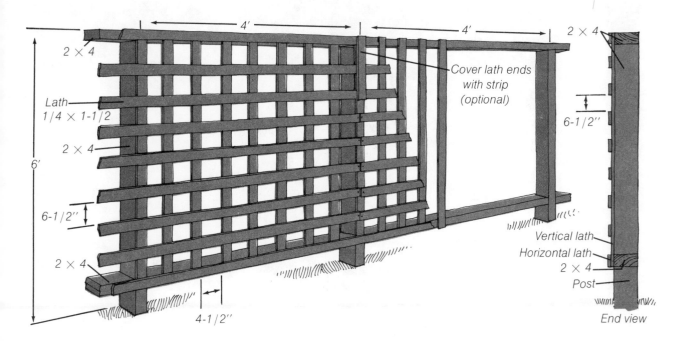

2 × 4

4'

4'

2 × 4

Cover lath ends
with strip
(optional)

2 × 4

Lath
1/4 × 1-1/2

2 × 4

6-1/2"

6'

6-1/2"

2 × 4

4-1/2"

Vertical lath
Horizontal lath
2 × 4
Post

End view

Some simple fences

Sometimes you may want to delineate a property line or an area on your property without the expense or even the appearance of a formal fence. And if you're plagued by people taking shortcuts, something simple put up across the path may still serve to discourage them.

All of the ideas shown can be built using the information in the chapters on planning (pages 4–17) and building basics (pages 48–60).

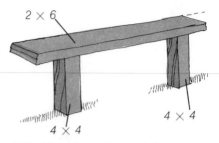

Rail of 2 by 6 set atop posts forms sturdy low fence, offers seating.

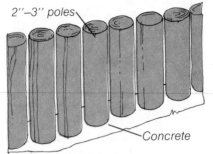

Poles set in concrete form solid barrier or low retaining wall.

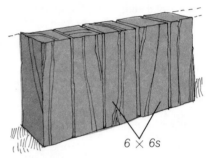

Low retainer consists of 6 by 6s sunk in ground, toenailed together.

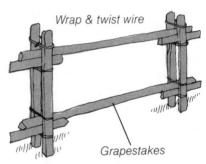

Diminutive post-and-rail of grapestakes makes inexpensive fence.

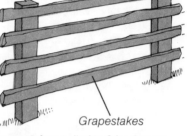

Grapestakes nailed to 2 by 4 posts make low, informal fence.

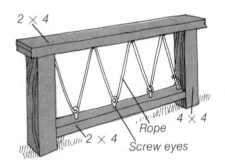

Heavy rope woven through screw eyes adds decorative touch to wood frame.

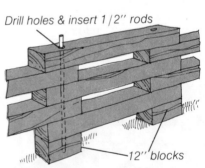

Stacked 4 by 4s fastened with steel rods make massive barricade.

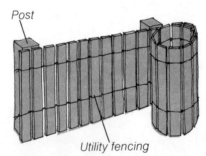

Utility fencing comes in rolls and goes up easily.

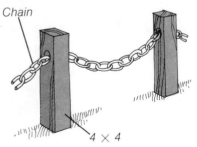

Heavy chain is threaded through posts; rope may be used instead.

Wire picket fencing serves as temporary or decorative border.

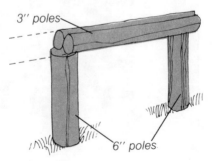

Small poles are nailed atop larger poles for low, rustic fence.

Garden screens

A screen is a short fence erected within the bounds of a piece of property to provide privacy, shade, shelter from the wind, a backdrop for plants, a barrier, or decoration. Often more lightly constructed than fences, screens may be permanent or movable.

With imaginative design and proper placement of screens, you can create a private world on your property without a penned-in feeling. By choosing from high and low, short and long, and open and solid screens, you can solve most of the problems in creating that private world.

Here are some of the things you can accomplish with screens:
• Create outdoor rooms by defining activity areas.
• Achieve separation of activity areas.
• Provide privacy for parties, quiet gatherings, and other outdoor entertaining.
• Hide unsightly utility yards, pool equipment, and garbage storage.
• Provide protection from wind.
• Control sunlight to create total shade, dappled shade, or filtered sunlight.
• Provide a background or support for plants or artwork.
• Create an illusion of quiet by visually blocking out sources of noise.

Though almost any type of fence shown in this book can be used as a screen, here we offer some specific ideas to help you with your garden planning. The dimensions shown can be adjusted to fit your particular needs. You'll find more ideas in the color section beginning on page 18. Information to help you plan your screen begins on page 4. For techniques to help you build it, check the section that begins on page 48.

DECORATIVE SCREEN

1 × 2
1 × 2
Wire mesh
2 × 4 (bolt or screw to posts)
4 × 4
2 × 4

PORTABLE PLASTIC PANEL SCREEN

4'
6'
1 × 2
2 × 2
Planter box
Plastic panel
Planter box
Casters

PLASTIC SCREEN

12''
12''
12''
12''
15''
2 × 4
2 × 2
4 × 4
2 × 2
4 × 4
Plastic screening between horizontal & vertical 2 × 2s
2 × 4

CANVAS SCREEN

1 × 2s
1 × 4
6'
2'
2'
2 × 2
Tacks
1 × 2
Canvas
1 × 4
2 × 4

HEAVY TRELLIS SCREEN

8'
8'
2 × 4
4 × 4

SLATTED SCREEN

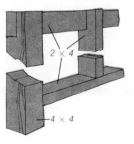
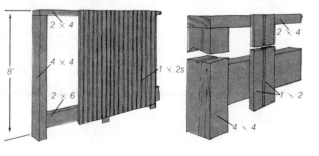

8'
2 × 4
4 × 4
2 × 6
1 × 2s
2 × 4
1 × 2
4 × 4

MAINTENANCE, REPAIR & DECORATION

- *Maintaining your fence*
- *Repairing your fence*
- *Decorating an existing fence*

Fence ailments—their causes and cures—may be found in this chapter, along with tips on keeping your fence in good condition and improving its appearance. Even sturdy, well-built fences require periodic maintenance; fences get damaged, and older ones will show their age. In either case, you can probably do the repair work yourself.

MAINTAINING YOUR FENCE

If you want your fence to live a long life, give it an annual checkup, preferably in the spring while the ground is soft but not too muddy.

First, check the posts for rot. The first signs of decay usually appear on posts at ground level, or a few inches below it. Dig around the post about 4 inches below ground level and check it for rot with a pocket knife, ice pick, or other sharp, pointed tool. If the blade penetrates the wood easily, rot has set in and the post will have to be repaired or replaced.

In some cases, the post will be so rotted that a quick visual inspection will tell the whole story.

Check post alignment with a carpenter's level to make sure that all posts are still plumb. Over the years, posts sink or tilt because of unstable soil, frost heaving, or wind action. To remedy the problem, you'll first have to realign the posts, and then reset them. You'll find directions on pages 81–82.

Next, check for loose rails and siding; renail if necessary, using good quality, galvanized nails. If boards or rails have aged to the point where they split when nailed, you'll have to replace them with new ones.

If you have plantings against the fence, look for tendrils, shoots, or small branches that have worked themselves into fence joints where they will pry apart the fence.

You can extend the life of an unpainted wood fence by annually coating all above-ground surfaces with a water sealer. If the fence is painted or stained, check the condition of the finish; reapply finish if necessary.

On metal fences or fence parts, remove any rust with a commercial rust remover and apply a rust resistant finish to the metal.

REPAIRING YOUR FENCE

Fence repair most often means repairing or replacing posts, simply because they are the most likely to decay, or to be thrown out of alignment by wind action, unstable soil, or merely the weight they must carry. Misaligned posts can loosen rails and siding materials, causing further damage like warping or splitting.

It is best to repair or replace decaying posts before they rot completely through. When a post loses its structural strength because of rot, it not only fails to hold up its share of the fence, but it adds its own weight to the burden that neighboring posts must support. Deterioration of a whole section of fence can proceed rapidly from this point.

Depending on the condition of your fence, and the nature of the damage, you can effect repairs using one of the following methods:

Repairing rotted posts

When posts are rotted at or below ground level, the repair method illustrated above right is the most effective and visually acceptable, provided the above-ground portion of the post is still sound. Posts rotted in this manner are rarely removed entirely, not only because removal is difficult, but also because rails and siding can be damaged while detaching them from posts.

Here's how:

1. Dig around rotted post to a depth of 2½ feet below ground level. If post is set in concrete, use a pick or wrecking bar to break up concrete and remove it.

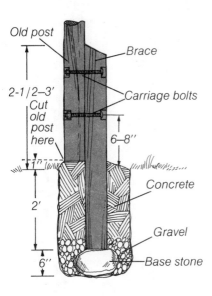

2. Cut post off 1 inch above ground level and remove all rotted wood from hole. *Do not* detach rails and siding from post.

3. From pressure-treated lumber or heartwood of a decay-resistant species (like redwood) with same dimensions as post, cut a brace about 5 feet long, with top cut at a 45° angle (to allow water runoff).

4. Use ½-inch-diameter carriage bolts with nuts and washers to attach brace to post, as shown in drawing. Bottom bolt should be 6 to 8 inches above ground level and penetrate sound wood in post.

5. Set brace in concrete and gravel as shown, angling top of pour to allow water runoff. Use a 2-foot level to align post vertically before concrete sets.

Adding new posts

If most or all of the posts are rotten, or if they're damaged above ground level, install new posts midway between them as illustrated above right. This method is also used when the fence design makes repairs on existing posts impractical.

For appearance's sake, new posts should be centered exactly midway between old ones. Do not remove old posts or you'll weaken the fence considerably.

Here's how:

1. Mark positions for new posts at center directly under bottom rail; dig holes 2½ feet deep. Make sure holes are in line with existing posts.

2. Cut new posts so they can be set 2 feet deep, with their tops butted firmly against underside of top rail. (For post-and-board fences, set new posts the same height as old ones and simply attach siding.)

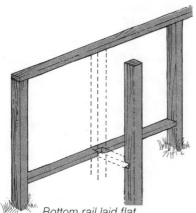

Bottom rail laid flat

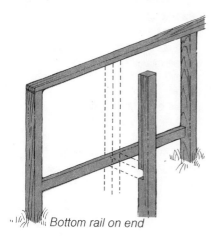

Bottom rail on end

3. If lower rail on fence is a 2 by 4 placed flat, cut a groove ("dado") in both rail and post to form an interlocking joint when post is slipped into place, as shown above. If bottom rail is set on edge, you need only notch the post.

4. Slip new post in place; check vertical alignment with a level and then nail rails and siding to post.

5. Set new post in concrete, following instructions on page 54.

Recheck vertical alignment and adjust post before concrete sets.

Replacing existing posts

Sometimes removing the post entirely and replacing it with a new one is the only practical repair method; either the old post is damaged above ground, or the fence design would look unattractive with an added or repaired post. If you do replace a post, take care when removing nails so you do not damage the rails and siding.

Here's how:

1. Cut old post off at ground level and carefully detach upper part from rails and siding.

2. Dig out underground portion of post, making sure you remove all pieces of rotted wood from hole. If post has been set in concrete, use a pick or wrecking bar to break concrete into manageable chunks for removal.

3. Dig out hole to proper depth (see page 53 to determine this) and slip new post into place.

4. Secure rails and siding to new post, using good quality, galvanized nails (do *not* drive new nails into existing nail holes). If rails and siding tend to split easily when being nailed, predrill new nail holes, using a bit slightly smaller in diameter than nail shank.

5. Set new post in concrete and gravel, following directions on page 54. With a level, align post vertically before concrete sets.

Resetting sound posts

Wind action, shifting soil, and frost heaving may throw posts out of plumb, causing the fence to lean and loosening rails and siding. If the posts are sound (no rot present), they can be realigned and reset in a stronger concrete setting.

Here's how:

1. Dig out around post to a depth several inches above its bottom. For posts set in concrete, expose concrete to bottom of pour.

2. Push post back into alignment and brace with a 2 by 4 as shown in drawing below. If post is too hard to push by brute strength, you'll need the aid of a device called a "come-along" (see drawing) to pull post into alignment. Come-alongs are available at tool rental shops.

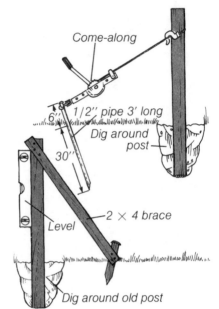

Come-along

6" — *1/2" pipe 3' long*

Dig around post

30"

Level

2 × 4 brace

Dig around old post

3. When post is aligned with other posts and plumbed, pour concrete into hole; tamp firmly, sloping surface away from post to divert rain; and let set for at least 48 hours before removing brace and reattaching rails and siding.

Repairing wind-damaged fences

If a prevailing wind has either damaged your fence or pushed posts out of alignment, the fence will need additional bracing after you make repairs, so that the problem doesn't recur.

Brace posts as shown in the drawing above right. Or you can add small offshoot fences to the side away from the wind, to brace the fence.

If the fence is a solid design (panels, butted boards, or lapped boards), consider making openings in it by removing a few boards or

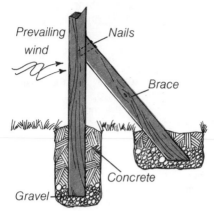

Prevailing wind

Nails

Brace

Concrete

Gravel

cutting openings in panels to reduce wind pressure against the fence.

Replacing rails or siding

Carefully measure all dimensions of original rails or siding before buying replacements.

When pulling off parts to be replaced, be careful not to damage those you wish to save; as they tear out, old nails can split wood. Use galvanized nails to attach new fence members; do not drive them into existing nail holes. Use a carpenter's framing square to square rails to posts before joining them.

On bare wood fences, the color of the new wood most likely won't match the old. You can give new wood an aged look by following the "aging method" described on page 59.

DECORATING AN EXISTING FENCE

Many homeowners find themselves confronted with dull, ordinary fences or sometimes with the "ugly side" of a neighbor's fence. But these are problems that yield to solutions. Aside from the planting ideas beginning on page 84, there are a number of other ways to add visual interest to your fence.

A few decorating ideas are presented here; with some thought and creativity, you can adapt them to your fence or come up with unique ideas of your own. Keep in

FENCE FACE LIFTS

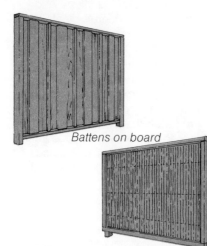

Battens on board

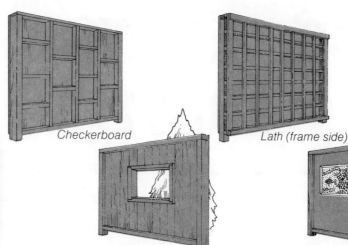

Checkerboard

Lath (frame side)

Reed or bamboo (frame side)

Window

Decorative panel

mind that your modifications shouldn't add much weight to your fence, as it was designed to carry a specific load. To stand up under the addition of heavy materials, your fence will require additional bracing unless it's exceptionally sturdy.

Before you start, be sure to make any needed repairs to put your fence in first-class condition.

Dressing up fence posts

As shown below, some pieces of wood and a few saw cuts can spruce up a prosaic fence post. Use one of these treatments, or let your eyes wander through the color section. For other ideas, keep a sharp eye during your daily travels.

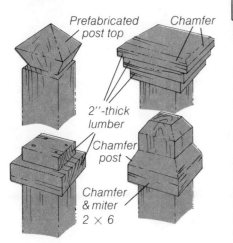

Prefabricated post top

Chamfer

2''-thick lumber

Chamfer post

Chamfer & miter 2 × 6

Give your fence a face lift

The most noticeable part of a fence is the face; here are several ideas for giving yours a new look (see drawings at top of page and below).

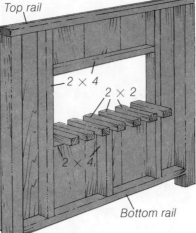

Top rail

2 × 4

2 × 2

2 × 4

Bottom rail

For more ideas, browse through the color section beginning on page 17 and through the projects that begin on page 61.

Give new life to the fence top

A roof or grillwork installed along the top of a fence will completely change the appearance of an ordinary structure. So will a 2 by 6 or short cross-pieces of 2 by 2 fastened to the top rail.

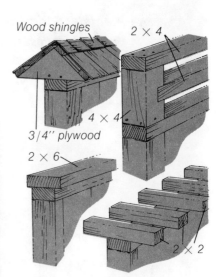

Wood shingles

2 × 4

4 × 4

3/4'' plywood

2 × 6

2 × 2

If your fence is sturdy and within your property line, mount a planter box behind it and let plants cascade down the face.

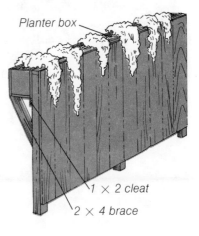

Planter box

1 × 2 cleat

2 × 4 brace

PLANTING & LIGHTING

- *Plants and the fence*
- *Lighting your fence*

Without plants around it, a fence can look flat and friendless. And without a fence nearby, plants can seem stranded. In other words, plants and fences go together.

Plants provide living patterns, textures, and colors that conceal or soften the sterner lines of a fence. Leafy vines or espaliered plants can work with an open-design fence to shade a section of garden from the afternoon sun. A fence can furnish support for vines and planters and a backdrop against which to train decorative shrubs.

At night, lights can give a new dimension to a fence and the plantings around it, accenting decorative shrubs. Plants viewed in silhouette against a lighted fence cast an entrancing pattern of shadows on the fence.

The fence and the environment

A fence or screen can alter the entire environment of your garden. The nature of the change will depend on the design and orientation of the fence or screen.

Sun and shade. For plants to thrive against a fence, they must be planted where they'll receive the right amount of sun and shade for their species. But plants that can normally withstand full sun may literally bake when grown against structures facing west or south, especially those painted white or some other light color.

One way of avoiding such a heat trap is to allow for air circulation around the plants. Either plant them several feet away from the fence or arrange for air circulation through the fence itself—for example, you can remove a few fence boards near the shrubs.

If the fence runs east to west, the north side will be shady; choose shade-loving plants for that side. The east side of a fence running north to south will be cooler than the west side; it can provide an ideal place for plants that thrive in partial sunlight.

The winter wind. A fence or screen can not only protect people against winds during the seasons of outdoor living; it can also protect plants against the chill winds of winter (see page 7). By deflecting icy winds, the fence or screen lessens the chance of frost damage to nearby plants. At the same time, it can trap and reflect heat on its sunny side, allowing you to grow plants that might not otherwise survive winter frost.

PLANTS AND THE FENCE

A fence can provide a backdrop for decorative plants or, if you desire, be camouflaged by plants. Fences furnish needed support to vines and espaliers. If you have an open or rail fence, plants growing on one side will appear on the other. Container plants, too, can find homes on fences.

Let a vine climb your fence

Climbing vines quickly adorn new fences and screens with foliage. Though a few will cling to a solid fence (notably Boston and English ivies), most vines require openwork—such as lattice, trellis, or fence rails—on which to climb (see drawings below). Vines that are not climbers must be tied to the fence.

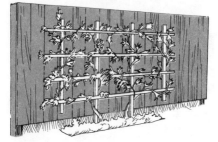

With open fences, double effect

Plants started on one side of an open fence soon grow through and appear on the other side. In effect, you get double coverage when you plant against picket, rail, wire mesh, or other open types of fences.

Camouflaging the fence

If yours is an uninteresting fence that you prefer not to see, use plants to hide it. Plants can completely obscure a fence or soften

its lines so that it blends with the landscape (see below).

In addition to the ideas shown, you can use vines (see left) and espaliers (see page 87) to camouflage your fence.

Hang plants on the fence

The fence itself can be a good place for plants. You can hang potted plants any number of ways—from simple brackets to a collector's item mounted on the fence. One example is an old ox yoke, as shown below.

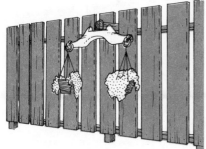

Shelves attached to the fence can support potted plants; the pots can stand free or be set into holes cut into the shelves. Fasten the shelves to the fence with heavy-duty commercial brackets, or else make your own of wood to match the shelves and the fence.

fence (see page 83); then use wire mesh and moss to hold soil in the recesses and provide a happy home for flowering plants or succulents.

get lost in the surrounding vegetation (see below). An especially dramatic treatment of decorative plants is the espalier.

If your fence is redwood, cedar, cypress, or a pressure-treated wood, you can build a checker-board onto the back side of your

Use your fence as a backdrop

Decorative shrubs and plants often appear at their best when displayed against a fence or screen. Bold leaves and interesting shapes don't

THE ART OF ESPALIER

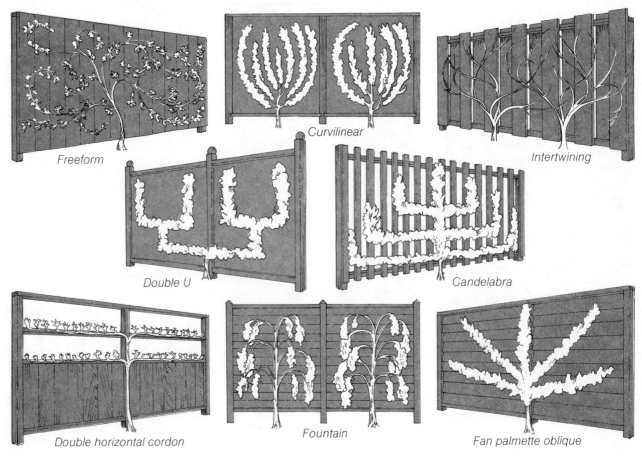

Freeform

Curvilinear

Intertwining

Double U

Candelabra

Double horizontal cordon

Fountain

Fan palmette oblique

The art of espaliering. An espalier is a tree or shrub trained against a trellis, fence, screen, or other support so that its trunk and branches, lying in a flat plane, create an artistic pattern. Placed against a fence or screen, shrubs and trees can be espaliered into shapes that add interest to a bare surface (see facing page).

Espaliers grow well in narrow planting spaces along a fence, or you can grow them in containers. They require careful pruning, done with an eye for detail and artistic balance. Many nurseries carry espaliers already started and trained by professionals, saving you the trouble of initial training.

To espalier against a fence, you must give a plant support; wire or wood lath, spaced 4″ to 6″ away from the fence, is most often used. The spacing allows air circulation around the plant. Use soft materials such as strips of cloth or plastic plant ties to fasten the plants in place.

Wire

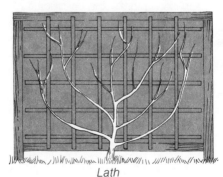
Lath

For detailed instructions on pruning and trimming espaliers, consult the *Sunset Pruning Handbook.*

LIGHTING YOUR FENCE

A few well-placed lights around your fence can create almost any nighttime mood you want. The terms used by landscape architects and designers for the different types of lighting—uplighting, down-lighting, texture lighting, area lighting, moonlighting, and silhouetting, to name just a few—will give you an idea of the possibilities. A few of the more useful types of fence lighting are illustrated below.

Uplighting. A single spotlight directed up into a shrub will silhouette some of the leaves and make others seem to glow. The spotlight can be concealed by low vegetation or behind the shrub.

Lighting an art object. Particularly near entryways and sitting areas, a fence can make a good stand or backdrop for displaying mosaics, carvings, and other art objects. Soft lighting directed upward from one side can provide flattering illumination and produce shadows that reveal the art object in detail.

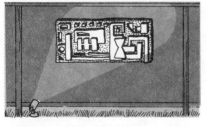

Silhouetting. One of the best-known and easiest lighting effects to produce, silhouetting is particularly effective if you have plants with dramatic leaves or interesting shapes. Light is directed away from

the plant and toward a fence close behind.

Lighting for shadow effects. Plant shadows on a fence at night can create a fantasy of shapes. By placing the source of light close to the planting and directing the light upward from the ground, you can make the shadows appear large and dramatic. A wide-beamed light spreads the light so that interesting shadows appear on the fence while soft light illuminates the planting.

Experiment with lighting. You can hire a professional to design your lighting system, or you can do it yourself by experimenting with different lighting effects. To do that experimenting, you'll need a clamp-on lamp or two, extension cords, and flood and spotlight bulbs. Buy bulbs of several wattages so that you can evaluate lighting levels.

A few words of caution: Work only when the weather is fair and the ground dry underfoot. And don't let your temporary lighting linger and become permanent.

There are many possibilities for lighting your fence. Take time to work out the effect you want, and you'll save time and money—and disappointment—later on. You'll find information on outdoor lighting and wiring in the *Sunset* book *Basic Home Wiring Illustrated.*

PLANNING & BUILDING GATES

If good fences make good neighbors, then good gates make good impressions. A front gate—the first thing visitors encounter—tells something about the people who live beyond it. The visual message can be inviting or forbidding, formal or informal, elaborate or functional.

Other gates on the property can also affect the atmosphere surrounding the house and garden. All gates must be carefully designed to give the visual cues you intend.

PLANNING YOUR GATE

When planning your gate, there are a number of details to be considered. The gate's location, size, and style, the material it's made of, even its latch and hinges—all combine to create that first impression. So each detail should be worked out to your satisfaction before you begin to build.

Choosing the location

Gates are located for convenience. In most instances, that location will be obvious; for example, a gate will be needed in a proposed fence where it intersects a walk or driveway. In new landscaping, gate locations are dictated by the overall landscape plan.

If you're faced with a choice of several locations along the fence line, give thought to present foot-traffic patterns and how the gate will affect them. Consider also any proposed landscaping or structural changes to the yard that may alter traffic through it, and locate the gate accordingly.

Determining gate size

The dimensions of your gate will be determined by the height of the fence it serves and the width of the walk, path, or driveway it must span. When figuring the width of the gate opening, think about the type of traffic that must pass through it.

Walk-through gates should pro-

- *Planning your gate*
- *Building your gate*
- *Maintaining and repairing your gate*

vide adequate clearance for yard maintenance equipment (wheelbarrows, garden tractors, and the like), garden furniture, and other large items that are periodically moved through the entry. Few things are more irritating than skinning your knuckles on the gate posts when pushing a wheelbarrow through the gate opening.

Driveway gates should provide clearance for large trucks as well as for cars. A possible solution for wide openings is a double gate, especially if your design calls for solid, heavy gate construction.

If you're planning a driveway gate, consider installing an electric gate operator, both for security purposes and convenience (see page 91 for details).

How will it open?

Your gate can either swing or slide open. Commonly used for driveways, sliding gates operate either on wheels, or on rollers attached to a track set into the ground. A few types are suspended on an overhead track, but these are usually not suitable for driveways because of the low overhead clearance.

Your other option is a swinging gate, either double or single.

Direction of swing. Your choice of the direction in which the gate swings will be influenced by both the location of the gate and the design of the fence or wall on which it's hung. Here are a few guidelines:

• Entry gates usually swing inward, toward the house or driveway; likewise, gates in boundary fences swing into your property. A gate on your property can swing in the direction of greater traffic flow.

• On sloped ground, hang gates to swing toward the downhill side if possible, to avoid having to cut the gate bottom to the slope angle (see page 92).

• If a single gate is located at the corner of a fence, it should swing back against the corner so it is out

of the way when open (see drawing below).

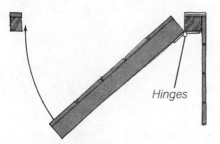

Hinges

• If both gate and its posts are the same thickness, the gate can swing in either direction.

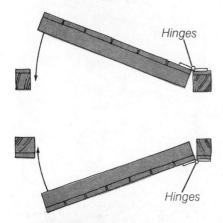

Hinges

Hinges

• Gates with very wide posts, such as those set in masonry walls, are usually centered and can be hinged to swing in either direction (see drawing below). If you align the gate with one side of the post or the other, the gate should swing open on that side. Opening it in the other direction will require a wide, unsightly gap on the latch side so that the gate will clear the latch post.

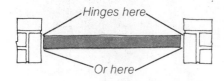

Hinges here

Or here

• For safety, a gate should be placed only at the top of a flight of steps, not at the bottom, and should swing away from the steps. This way, pedestrians will have to stop to open the gate and become aware of the steps beyond before pitching down them.

Selecting a style

Your own taste is your best guide to a gate design you can live with. Your choice, though, should be influenced by the styles of surrounding structures, particularly the fence or wall in which the gate will be set. For example, an ornamental iron gate may accent a brick wall perfectly but look quite out of place in a rustic split rail fence.

Gates can either match a fence or contrast with it. Inconspicuous gates are sometimes built for security reasons, but more often because an obtrusive design would cause an unattractive break in the fence line.

Conversely, a gate can be designed to call attention to itself in order to lead visitors to the proper entrance. Front entry gates are often showpieces, reflecting the artistic tastes (and sometimes talents) of their owners.

A number of attractive gate designs appear on pages 44–47 in the color section.

Selecting hardware and materials

Gates get more wear and abuse than any other part of a fence or wall. If they're to last, gates must be built solidly and attached with top-quality, heavy-duty hardware.

Materials. For the most part, the gate material you choose will be metal or wood.

Metal gates include chain link or ornamental metal (wrought iron, aluminum, or tubular steel) types. All metal gates are prefabricated, either in stock designs available from gate manufacturers, or custom made to your specifications. Metal gate fabricators may be found in the Yellow Pages under the headings "Gates" or "Iron, Ornamental Work."

Wood gates, on the other hand, can be designed and built by a homeowner with moderate carpentry skills. Or you can hire a carpenter or fence contractor to build the gate, either from your plans or theirs.

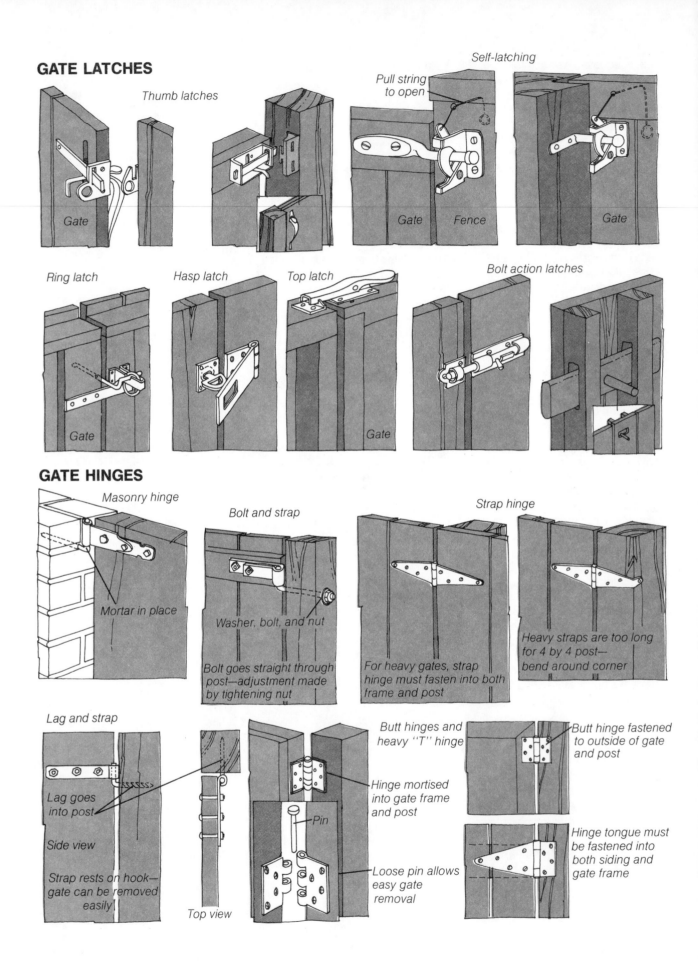

GATE LATCHES

Thumb latches

Self-latching

Pull string to open

Gate

Gate   Fence

Gate

Ring latch

Gate

Hasp latch

Top latch

Gate

Bolt action latches

GATE HINGES

Masonry hinge

Mortar in place

Bolt and strap

Washer, bolt, and nut

Bolt goes straight through post—adjustment made by tightening nut

Strap hinge

Heavy straps are too long for 4 by 4 post— bend around corner

For heavy gates, strap hinge must fasten into both frame and post

Lag and strap

Lag goes into post

Side view

Strap rests on hook— gate can be removed easily

Top view

Pin

Butt hinges and heavy "T" hinge

Hinge mortised into gate frame and post

Loose pin allows easy gate removal

Butt hinge fastened to outside of gate and post

Hinge tongue must be fastened into both siding and gate frame

In selecting materials for wood gates, you have the same choices as in fences. Most gates have diagonally braced frames made from 2 by 4s covered with facing material. Lighter frames (made from 2 by 2s or 2 by 3s) can be used if the siding is exterior plywood, hardboard, or some other sheet material. Siding made of sheet material usually needs no diagonal bracing, as the material itself serves to keep the frame square.

Lumber used for a gate frame should be straight and free of defects (for information on selecting lumber, see pages 15–17). Even slightly warped lumber can throw a whole gate out of alignment. Choose a wood that has been pressure-treated with a preservative, or all-heart lumber from a decay-resistant species, such as redwood, red cedar, or cypress.

If you must buy green or damp lumber, let it dry out thoroughly before using it (see page 50).

Latches. Because the latch is the device people reach for to open and close the gate, it is often the focal point in the gate design. So it's a good idea to consider carefully the appearance as well as mechanical operation of the latch.

Not all latches are suitable for every gate. You must either choose a latch that works with your gate design, or, if you've found a latch that suits your fancy, adapt the gate design to work with the latch. Hardware stores and home improvement centers carry latches.

The drawings at left illustrate the most commonly used gate latches. You can special order more ornate styles or have a custommade latch fabricated by a metal worker. If you're building a wood gate, you can devise a wooden latch like one in the drawing or create your own design.

Though latches usually serve to keep a gate closed, some can hold the gate open. The drawings at right show two types that do this.

Whether you buy a latch or make your own, be sure it is sturdy enough for the gate and the rough

handling it will have to take. Use the longest screws or bolts possible when attaching the latch assembly.

Like other hardware for fences and gates, latches should be rust and corrosion resistant.

Electric gate operators. On driveway gates, electric gate operators are installed for both security and convenience. Similar in principle to the electric garage door opener, these devices can be operated by a switch in the house (usually in conjunction with a two-way intercom), a keyed switch outside the gate, radio controls inside a car, or a combination of these. Models are available for single and double swinging gates and sliding gates.

Electric locking devices can also be installed on walk-through gates. These, too, employ keyed switches by the gate, and remote-controlled switches with intercoms so house occupants can be selective about visitors.

You'll find electric gate operators listed in the Yellow Pages under "Door Operating Devices." The dealer you choose can recommend the best unit for your gate.

LATCHING A GATE OPEN

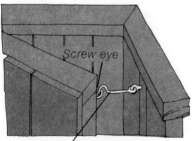
Screw eye

Eye hook (corner)

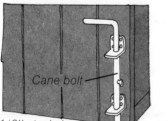
Cane bolt

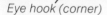
1/2" steel pipe driven into ground (or drill hole in concrete)

Hinges. The principal cause of gate failure is inadequate hinges. It is better to use an overly strong hinge than one not strong enough.

The nature of your gate siding will influence your choice of hinge. It would be impossible, for example, to mount heavy strap hinges on a gate paneled in translucent plastic.

Sometimes you'll want to buy hinges that match the latch, and this may call for a revision in the gate design.

If a fence is used to confine small children, self-closing hinges are a worthwhile investment; springs in the hinge mechanism automatically close the gate, which otherwise might be left ajar by visitors.

Some of the more familiar hinges are illustrated on the facing page. All of them do a good job, provided they are sized for the weight of the gate and attached with screws that are long enough. Many packaged hinges include fasteners that are too short for a heavy gate. Use screws that go as far into the wood as possible, without coming out the other side. It's best to put three hinges on gates over 5 feet tall or more than 3 feet wide unless you use heavy-duty hinges. A knowledgeable hardware dealer can assist you in choosing the right sized hinges for your gate. Hinges should be rust and corrosion resistant.

Putting plans on paper

Once you've planned your gate—style, size, location, basic material, and types of hardware—make a detailed drawing of it. This will help you in ordering materials and, later, in building the gate. A typical drawing is shown on the next page.

Your drawing should include the following specifications:

• Height of gate posts and distance between them.

• Overall dimensions of the gate itself. Also indicate clearance space between the gate and gate posts on both latch and hinge

TYPICAL GATE

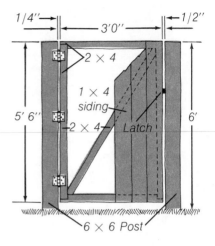

- 1/4″
- 3′0″
- 1/2″
- 2 × 4
- 1 × 4 siding
- 5′6″
- 2 × 4
- Latch
- 6′
- 6 × 6 Post

sides. (To estimate clearances, see "Building the gate frame" above right).

- Dimensions of individual framing and siding pieces.
- Positions of latch, hinges, and other hardware.

Now you can make an accurate list of materials you'll need and order them from your building supplier.

BUILDING YOUR GATE

Building your own gate can be a satisfying form of creative expression—everyone who walks through it must pause temporarily to look at your work. Simple and unadorned or a work of art, your gate will be on display and can reflect your care for craftsmanship.

The normal gate construction sequence is to (1) set and align gate posts, (2) build the frame, (3) add siding, (4) hang the gate, and (5) install the latch.

For the most part, these procedures are quite simple, but they do require precise workmanship. A few miscalculations in gate post alignment, or in measuring, cutting, and assembling gate components, will result in a gate that won't open and close smoothly. Posts must be set firmly in concrete or they'll soon lean, hampering smooth gate operation. The gate must also be

built solidly and attached firmly to the post with heavy-duty hinges, or it will start to sag and bind soon after installation.

If you feel the required carpentry is beyond your ability, especially if your design calls for detailed joinery work, you can get help from a fence contractor or a carpenter with gate-building experience.

Setting and aligning gate posts

Gate posts must be set deeper than fence line posts because of the added stress placed upon them. They must also be lined up perfectly and plumbed vertically so that their inside faces are exactly parallel (see drawing below).

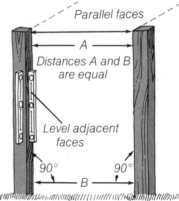

Parallel faces

A

Distances A and B are equal

Level adjacent faces

90° 90°

B

Set posts at least 1/3 their total length into the ground (for a 6-foot-tall gate, use 9-foot posts sunk 3 feet). All gate posts should be set in concrete.

Use a level to plumb posts vertically; then measure the space between the posts at both top and bottom to make sure the distances are equal, as shown in the drawing above. If the ground slopes between one gate post and the other, use a level and string to get an accurate bottom measurement between the posts. For more complete details on setting and aligning posts, see pages 54–56.

If you're attaching a gate to existing posts or pillars, make sure they, too, are in alignment. Plumb and reset, if necessary.

Building the gate frame

The frame is the skeleton that supports the body weight of the gate. So the type of frame you build will depend on both the size and weight of the siding it must support. Almost all gate frames need cross-bracing to keep the gate square and to prevent sagging (exceptions are gates with plywood or other rigid sheet siding). Bracing can be a diagonal wood piece or a wire and turnbuckle assembly, as discussed on the next page.

When determining gate size, plan the frame width to allow clearance space on both the hinge and latch sides of the gate. For gates with standard 2 by 4 framing and 4 by 4 posts, leave 1/2 inch between the latch post and the gate frame so the gate will swing without binding. The space on the hinge side will depend on the type of hinges you're using; for most standard hinges, 1/4 inch is sufficient.

If the ground slopes between posts (see drawing below), the bottom of the frame should *not* follow the slope angle; rather it should be at a 90° angle to the posts so the frame is perfectly square.

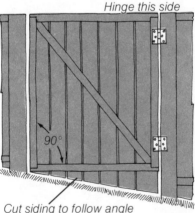

Hinge this side

90°

Cut siding to follow angle

When you apply the siding, you can cut it to follow the slope only if you hinge the gate on the downhill side, as shown in the drawing above. If you hinge it on the uphill side, cut the bottom of the siding so it won't scrape the ground when the gate is opened.

Bracing. The two accepted ways to brace a gate are shown in the drawings below. The first is to run a piece of wood diagonally from the bottom of the hinge side to the top of the latch side. The second is to run a metal wire and turnbuckle assembly in the opposite direction; from the bottom of the latch side to the top of the hinge side.

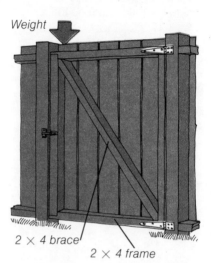

2 × 4 brace

2 × 4 frame

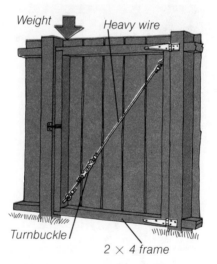

Turnbuckle

2 × 4 frame

The wood brace may harmonize with your gate design more than the wire and turnbuckle and will provide additional nailing surface for wood siding; the wire assembly is easier to install, weighs less, and can be adjusted if the gate sags.

Wire and turnbuckle assemblies are available at home improvement centers; they attach to the gate with large eye screws as shown.

For details on installing wood bracing, see step 3 below.

The step-by-step sequence below shows how to build a simple gate frame out of 2 by 4s. The overall dimensions and the lumber sizes can be changed to suit a number of gate designs.

The following are the basic steps for building a simple gate frame from 2 by 4s and attaching siding to it. The frame shown here is suitable for gates up to 6 feet tall and 3 feet wide; larger gates require heavier framing members. For details on attaching the siding, see below, and on hanging the gate, see page 94.

1. *Determine the gate size.* To determine the width of the gate, first measure the space between the gate posts at both top and bottom of the opening. (If it varies more than ¼ inch, you'll have to reset the posts before you can hang the gate.) Subtract ¾ inch from this measurement (to allow for gate swing clearance) to get the gate width. The height of your gate will be determined by both the height of the opening and your gate design.

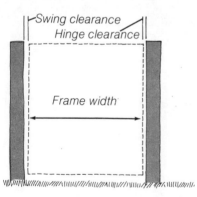

Swing clearance
Hinge clearance
Frame width

2. *Construct the frame.* Unless you want the gate siding to extend past the outside edges of the frame, you'll be building the frame to the width and height you determined in step 1.

Cut the frame pieces to proper lengths and assemble them on a workbench or other flat surface. Pieces can either be butted together or, for a stronger joint,

dadoed as shown in the drawing below.

For an even stronger joint, fasten the pieces with wood screws and exterior grade wood glue instead of nails. Use a carpenter's square to keep the pieces at right angles while joining them.

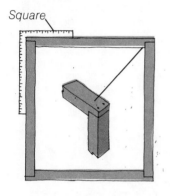

Square

3. *Attach the diagonal brace.* Double check squareness of the frame before you begin. Place the frame on a 2 by 4 (to be used for brace) and pencil in cutting marks on the brace as shown. For a tight fit, saw the brace to the *outside* of the pencil marks. Fasten the brace at each end by nailing through both horizontal and vertical rails. An alternative to a wooden brace is the wire and turnbuckle assembly (shown at left).

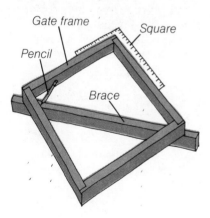

Gate frame
Square
Pencil
Brace

Attaching the siding

Cut the boards or pickets to size and lay them vertically across the frame, starting from the side where the hinge will go. If the last piece is not flush with the frame edge on the latch side, you'll have to either space the boards slightly or plane a little from one side of each board. (Though vertical boards are used here, horizontal and diagonal board sidings are similarly applied).

Before permanently attaching the boards, mark their positions on the frame; then nail the pieces starting from the hinge side, checking frequently with a square. The siding can overlap the latch side, if it is to act as a gate stop. (See right).

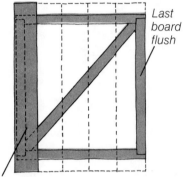

Last board flush

Start from hinge side

For plywood or other sheet siding, simply lay the frame flat over the siding, trace the outside edges with a pencil, and cut out the siding.

If the gate will be too heavy or awkward to lift with the siding attached, you can apply the siding after the frame is hung, provided the hinges have been attached to the back side of the frame where they won't interfere with the siding.

Hanging the gate

Attaching hinges is the first step in hanging your gate, and your first concern should be the size of the fasteners: screws should go into the frame and gate post as far as possible without coming out the other side. You may find the fasteners that come with the hinges too short. If so, replace them with longer ones of a corrosion resistant variety.

Predrill screw or bolt holes in frame with a bit that is slightly smaller than the diameter of the fasteners; then attach hinges to frame.

Once the hinges are on, hold the gate in place to check fit. If it is too close to the posts to swing freely, plane the edge of the latch side until it does fit. At this point either you can have a helper hold the gate in place or you can prop it in position with wood blocks or the like. Then mark the hinge and screw-hole positions on the post. Remove the gate and drill the holes; then replace the gate and attach the hinges to the post.

Once the gate is hung, make sure it swings easily, opens all the way, and closes flush with the posts. Make adjustments, if needed.

The next step is to install the latch assembly to the gate and corresponding post. Because the latch takes quite a beating, you should use long screws or bolts with it. They should be as long as possible without breaking through the other side.

Another way to build a gate

You can also build a gate in place. Some builders prefer this method, especially if a post is misaligned.

1. *Toenail the rails* to the posts, leaving the heads protruding so you can remove the nails later.

2. *Fasten the uprights* to the rails, putting ¼-inch plywood spacers between posts and uprights to provide clearance.

3. *Cut and fasten the brace*, making sure its bottom is on the hinge side.

4. *Install face-mounted hinges* using the longest screws that don't break through the far side.

5. *Nail the siding* to the frame.

6. *Remove the temporary nails* and saw off the rails flush with the uprights.

7. *Install the latch.*

Gate stop.

To complete the installation of your gate, attach a vertical strip of wood to the latch post to stop the gate when it closes; this keeps it from

swinging past its closed position and loosening its hinges.

The stop can be a strip of 1 by 1, 1 by 2, or 2 by 2, or it can be ½-inch door stop, depending on the proportions of your gate. The stop should run the full length of the gate, from top to bottom.

The siding on the fence or gate can also act as a stop by overlapping the gate frame on the latch side.

The drawings below show several common stops.

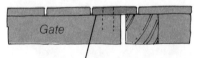

Nail gate stop to post

Gate

Stop

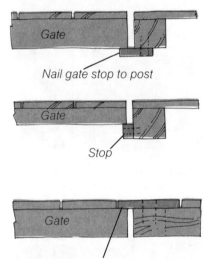

Siding on fence acts as stop

Gate

Siding on gate acts as stop

MAINTAINING AND REPAIRING YOUR GATE

Garden and entry gates normally take a severe beating. They're exposed to wind and weather, young gate swingers, and hurried people who push against the gate before the latch is free and slam the gate when they leave. Gates that are hung from badly set or insecure posts, or that contract and expand with the weather, often bind, refuse to latch, or scrape along the ground when opened.

If you regularly examine your gate and take care of any small problems as soon as you find them, you'll avoid the time and expense of making major repairs later on. Even though you check your gate on a regular basis, preferably when you check your fence and garden structures (see page 80), be sure to take care of any problems you notice during the year.

The drawing below illustrates some of the problems you may encounter when you check your gate. Read on for tips on maintaining and repairing your gate.

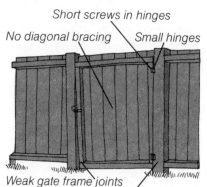

Short screws in hinges

No diagonal bracing   Small hinges

Weak gate frame joints

Posts not secure in ground

Hinges and latches. Hinge and latch screws have a way of working loose, especially if a gate gets heavy use. This may be normal; or it may indicate that the screws are too short, or that the hinges are too small or too few.

To tighten loose screws, first remove them and stuff the screw holes with steel wool soaked in woodworker's glue. While the glue is still wet, replace the screws.

If the screws come loose again, replace them with the longest possible screws that don't break through the wood on the back side, or else replace them with nuts and bolts.

Loose screws can also be a symptom of a gate with inadequate hinges. Gates more than 5 feet high or more than 3 feet wide should have three hinges. Two weak hinges can be strengthened with a third one of similar size, placed between the other two and a bit above the midpoint. Better yet, install three new hinges of the largest size that will fit on your gate. And don't forget to use the longest possible screws to attach them.

Sometimes, tightening the screws is not enough to make a latch work properly. If this is the case with your latch, make any other needed repairs to your gate (see below) before replacing or resetting the latch. Repairing a sagging gate or leaning fence post may correct the problem.

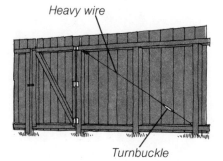

Heavy wire

Turnbuckle

Gate posts. A leaning hinge-side post is another major cause of trouble. It carries not only the weight of the gate, but also the weight of anyone swinging on it. If the post is tilting, you may be able to straighten it up and tamp the soil around it. But this will probably turn out to be a temporary remedy. If the post hasn't been set in concrete, it should be.

If the post has simply leaned over from the weight of the gate, you can straighten and hold it with a turnbuckle and heavy wire or threaded steel rod running to the bottom of another post along the fence line as shown in the drawing above right. This straightening method can also be used on the latch-side post.

The gate itself. Most gates aren't overly strong to begin with and will sag out of shape when subjected to weather. A gate may start to sag long before it begins binding: correcting the problem early will save major repairs later. Hinges, posts, or the gate itself may be the cause of the problem.

Tighten or replace loose hinges (see above). Check the posts and the gate with a level and square to determine if the sag is caused by a leaning post or is in the gate itself. If the post is leaning, read the section on gate posts.

A sagging gate with a wire and turnbuckle assembly can often be straightened with a few turns of the turnbuckle.

If the gate has a wood brace, square up the frame and renail the brace, frame, and siding. After rehanging it, your gate may still have a tired appearance, in which case you should add a wire and turnbuckle assembly. The wire and turnbuckle should run opposite to an existing diagonal wood brace (the wire should run from the top of the hinge side to the bottom of the latch side) to pull the gate back into place.

Turnbuckle kits, containing turnbuckle, heavy wire or threaded rods, and metal angle plates, are available at many hardware stores and home improvement centers (see page 93).

If the gate binds in wet weather, but works nicely during warm seasons, plane off a little of the latch post or the latch side of the gate frame to give at least a ¼-inch clearance for expansion. Conversely, if the gate shrinks so that the latch will not catch, you will have to either relocate the latch or replace it with one having a longer reach. If the gate has sunk straight down, simply reset the hinges and the latch.

The gate's finish. Because gates are subject to more wear and tear than the fences or walls surrounding them, they'll likely need more frequent refinishing. Wood gates have many joints that can trap moisture that causes decay. Give unfinished wood gates an annual coat of clear water-sealer; on painted gates, caulk joints and repaint when needed. For more information on finishes, see page 59.

To keep metal gates looking their best, remove rust or corrosion with a commercial rust remover and refinish with a rust-resistant paint.

INDEX